BARRY JACKSON

PHOTOSHOP
Cosmetic Surgery

A comprehensive guide to portrait retouching and body transforming

BARRY JACKSON

PHOTOSHOP
Cosmetic Surgery

A comprehensive guide to portrait retouching and body transforming

LARK BOOKS
A Division of Sterling Publishing Co., Inc.
New York

Photoshop Cosmetic Surgery
A Comprehensive Guide to Portrait Retouching and Body Transforming

10 9 8 7 6 5 4 3 2 1
First Edition

Library of Congress Cataloging-in-Publication Data

Jackson, Barry, 1963-
  Photoshop cosmetic surgery / Barry Jackson.-- 1st ed.
      p. cm.
  ISBN-10: 1-57990-800-4 (pbk.)
  ISBN-13: 978-1-57990-800-3
  1. Photography--Retouching. 2. Photography--Digital techniques. 3. Adobe
Photoshop. I. Title.
TR310.J33 2006
778.9'2--dc22

                         2005030171

Published by Lark Books, a division of
Sterling Publishing Co., Inc.
387 Park Avenue South, New York, N.Y. 10016

Copyright © The Ilex Press Limited 2006

This book was conceived by ILEX,
The Old Candlemakers, West Street, Lewes, BN7 1UP

Distributed in Canada by Sterling Publishing,
c/o Canadian Manda Group
165 Dufferin Street, Toronto, Ontario, Canada M6K 3H6

If you have questions or comments about this book, please contact:
Lark Books, 67 Broadway, Asheville, NC 28801, (828) 253-0467
www.larkbooks.com

Printed in China

ISBN: 13: 978-1-57990-800-3
ISBN: 10: 1-57990-800-4

For more information on this title, please visit:
www.web-linked.com/pcosus

For information about custom editions, special sales, premium and corporate
purchases, please contact Sterling Special Sales Department at 800-805-5489
or specialsales@sterlingpub.com.

CONTENTS

PHOTOSHOP Cosmetic Surgery

Welcome to the consulting rooms of the distinguished Photoshop surgeon, Dr. Barry Jackson, here assisted by his beautiful and talented senior staff nurse, Jane Peg. Dr. Jackson will act as your guide on a journey through the complex treatments and procedures employed by many of today's experts in the field of digital photography and image editing. This will take the form of an extensive series of Photoshop-based operations focusing exclusively on reshaping and transforming the human face and body.

The process will begin with a pre-operative consultation and a tour of the digital operating theater, including a detailed examination of the Photoshop surgeon's tool kit. Nurse J. Peg will be on hand to offer a range of non-surgical procedures and to administer expert advice on all matters cosmetic.

Dr. Jackson himself will answer the most commonly asked image-editing questions and prescribe the appropriate course of treatment for each case. Following diagnosis, the doctor will conduct a series of in-depth Photoshop tutorials, using both PC and Macintosh equipment. The resulting transformations are as sure to impress fellow beauticians and cosmetic surgeons—professionals and novices alike—as they are to delight the good doctor's patients.

So please come in, sit down, and make yourself comfortable. The doctor will see you shortly.

CONTENTS

SECTION 1

BEFORE
PHOTOGRAPHS

The Digital Operating Theater

A reference guide to the Photoshop workspace and the most
useful tools and features used by image retouchers

THEATRE OVERVIEW
The workspace and palettes

Before attempting even the simplest of operations, it is essential to have a basic working knowledge of the Photoshop interface. Over the next few pages I will take you on a guided tour of the Photoshop interface—or, as I like to call it, "The Digital Operating Theater." This will include an in-depth examination of the Photoshop tool kit, detailing the most useful tools and features available to the Photoshop cosmetic surgeon.

Taking a few minutes at this point to get acquainted with the working area will help significantly when following the tutorials in the remaining sections of the book. Alternatively, if you are already familiar with the Photoshop tools and interface, this section of the book can be viewed as a visual reference guide to be used as and when more information is required on a specific tool or feature.

The Photoshop interface consists of an active image area where images are opened and worked upon; a selection of floating windows, including the Toolbox; and a selection of info and navigation palettes. At the top, the Tool Options bar and a main menu bar contain a selection of drop-down menus. With all these objects it's not surprising that the workspace can occasionally seem rather cluttered. Luckily for us, Photoshop contains various options for tailoring the workspace to your own particular taste, and providing a more efficient and flexible working environment.

Menu bar

Found at the very top of the screen, the menu bar contains nine drop-down menus. Each one contains various sub-menus, allowing the user access to most of Photoshop's features and commands.

Tool Options bar

The Tool Options bar can be found at the top of the screen, attached to the main menu bar; from here, a choice of options relating to the currently selected tool may be adjusted to alter the tool's effects. If preferred, the Tool Options bar can be unhooked from the menu bar and docked at the bottom of the screen by dragging the gripper bar on its left edge.

Toolbox

The Toolbox is made up of a rectangular grid containing a series of icons, each representing a specific tool. These can be selected with a click of the mouse, or via the corresponding keyboard shortcut. Many of the icons contain a little black arrow at their bottom right corner. Click on this to access a pull-out menu containing alternative tools, or hold down the **Shift** key while pressing the corresponding keyboard shortcut to scroll through the group of tools. Once a tool is selected, you can change its attributes via the Tool Options bar at the top of the screen.

SHORTCUT   Hit the **F8** key to hide or show this group of palettes.

Info palette

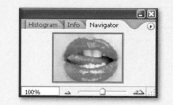

Docked with the Navigator and Histogram palettes, this displays information about the image currently being worked on. This includes RGB and CMYK info, along with the cursor's X and Y coordinates, and the height and width of any crop or selection applied to the image.

Navigator palette

This shows a small preview of the image being worked on. Adjust the slider at the bottom of the palette to zoom in or out of the main image. The visible area of the main image appears as a red frame on the preview image, and this frame can be moved around the preview to select the area of the main image you wish to work on.

Histogram palette

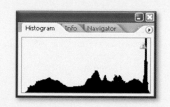

The Histogram palette is in the form of a graph that provides a visual representation of the tonal range of the active image. The default palette displays the composite RGB/CMYK levels, but this palette can be expanded to display the levels for each channel.

SHORTCUT   *Hit the **F6** key to hide or show this group of palettes.*

Color palette

Docked with the Swatches and Style palettes, this is used to set the foreground and background colors. You can do so by dragging the color sliders, or by clicking anywhere within the color field at the bottom of the palette.

Swatches palette

The Swatches palette is a set of preset colors. Click on any of these to select the foreground color, or click on the arrow at the top right of the palette to open a sub-menu from where new sets of color swatches can be selected.

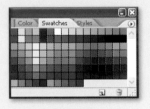

Styles palette

The Styles palette is a selection of preset combinations of stylized "layer effects," which can be applied to layers and text. New custom combinations of layer effects can be created and saved to the Styles palette.

SHORTCUT   *Hit the **F9** key to hide or show this group of palettes.*

Actions palette

Docked with the History palette, Actions are a selection of pre-recorded command sequences that allow you to apply a technique to an image automatically. It is possible to record your own actions, so if you have a lengthy technique that you often apply to images, record the commands as you run through them, save the "action," and then assign it a keyboard shortcut.

History palette

The History palette records each change applied to an image, allowing you to return to previous stages of the image before changes were made. By default the History palette records the last 20 image states, but this can be increased in the program's preferences. Any number of temporary Snapshots can also be created to allow you to return to key points in the editing process.

SHORTCUTS EXPLAINED

*Throughout this book you'll find keyboard shortcuts in the text. Learning these gives you the quick hands a successful surgeon needs. It doesn't matter where you do your surgery—whether it's on a Mac or a PC—since we show the equivalent keys seperated by a slash (/). For example, **Ctrl/⌘+Shift+Z** means PC users should hold the Control key (often marked "Ctrl") and the Shift key, and tap the Z key. Mac users would hold the Command key (marked ⌘ or ⌘) and the Shift key, and tap the Z key.*

SHORTCUT · *Hit the **F7** key to hide or show this group of palettes.*

SHORTCUT · *Hit the **Tab/→| key** to hide or show all open palettes.*

Layers palette

Docked with the Channels and Paths palettes, the Layers palette contains a list of all the layers, layer sets, and layer effects present in an active image. From here many tasks can be achieved such as creating, deleting, displaying, hiding, and copying layers.

Channels palette

Channels are grayscale images that store information about the image. The image's color mode determines the number of channels the image has—an RGB image, for example, has three channels: one red, one blue, and one green. A grayscale image has only one channel. Channels can be edited individually or even added to store information such as selections or masks.

Paths palette

Paths are outlines created using the Pen or Shape tools. They're vector based, so they don't use pixels and are not dependent on resolution when editing. Paths can be converted into selections by pressing **Ctrl/⌘+Return/↵**.

YOUR TOOLS
The Photoshop surgeon's tool kit

Using the right tools for the job has always been an essential requirement in any practical profession. You wouldn't find a mechanic tightening a bolt with a pair of tweezers, nor a heart surgeon performing a cardiac bypass with a knife and fork. Likewise, in the virtual world of Photoshop cosmetic surgery it is equally important to choose the right tool for the task in hand.

This at first may seem a daunting prospect given the range and complexity of tools available in Photoshop, but don't worry. In this section of the book I will perform a detailed examination of the most useful tools and features of the Photoshop surgeon's tool kit.

Making a selection

Undoubtedly the most common process in any Photoshop operation is the creation of selections. Selections are used to isolate a specific area of an image, allowing us to make adjustments to the area without affecting the remainder of the image. There are a number of tools that can be used to create selections, some being more suited to a particular type of image than others. Because of this, it is important to know which tools are available to you and their suitability for each procedure.

SHORTCUT   *Hit the **W** key to select the Magic Wand tool, or try holding down the **SHIFT** key while clicking with the mouse to add to the selection (holding down the **ALT/**⌥ key and clicking with the mouse subtracts from the selection).*

Magic Wand tool

The easiest selection tool to use, but not always the most reliable, the Magic Wand tool works by selecting areas with the same luminosity value. The Magic Wand tool is best suited to high-contrast flat color situations— for example, to select the background of a portrait taken against a plain backdrop, simply click on the plain backdrop to create an instant selection of the background. The tool's "tolerance" of color variation can be adjusted in the Tool Options bar, along with the option to add or subtract from the selection.

SHORTCUT Hit the **L** key to select the Lasso tool, or hold down the **SHIFT** key while repeatedly pressing the **L** key to scroll through the tool variations.

Freehand Lasso

To create a selection with the Freehand Lasso, hold down the mouse button as you draw around the area to be selected. Let go of the button to join the selection. This tool is suitable for quick selections where accuracy isn't important—for example, replacing closed eyes with open eyes from another photo. The amount of feathering (softness of the edges) can be set in the Tool Options bar.

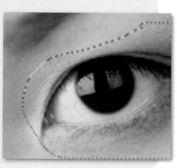

SHORTCUT When using the Polygon Lasso, hold down the **ALT/⌥** key to revert to Freehand Lasso mode (release the **ALT/⌥** key to return to Polygon Lasso mode).

Polygonal Lasso

To create a selection with the Polygonal Lasso, click to start the selection, then let go and position the mouse to create a straight line. Click the mouse to add another anchor point, let go, reposition the mouse, click, and so on. To complete the selection, click back on the start point. The Polygonal Lasso is the ideal tool for making selections around straight items such as boxes or buildings. The tool options are the same as those for the Freehand Lasso.

SHORTCUT Hit the **M** key to select the Rectangular Marquee tool, or hold down the **SHIFT** key while repeatedly pressing the **M** key to toggle between Rectangular and Elliptical modes.

Rectangle Marquee & Elliptical Marquee

To make a selection with the Rectangle or Elliptical Marquees, simply hold down the mouse button and drag. Hold down the **Shift** key while dragging to constrain your selection to a perfect square or circle, or hold down the **Alt/⌥** key to start the selection from the center rather than the corner. There are various tool options available, such as adding, subtracting, intersecting, and feathering the selection, as well as entering height and width measurements to create selections of a fixed size. The Marquee tools are best suited to quickly selecting parts of an image, such as pupils or irises, when changing color or fixing red eye.

SHORTCUT When using the Magnetic Lasso, hold down the **ALT** key to revert to Polygonal Lasso mode. Keep the **ALT/⌥** key depressed and hold down the mouse button to change to freehand mode. Releasing the **ALT/⌥** key returns to you Magnetic Lasso mode.

Magnetic Lasso

To create a selection with the Magnetic Lasso, click to start, and then draw around the outline of the object you wish to select. The tool detects changes in contrast in the image, laying down anchor points on the edge of the object as you move the mouse roughly along the edge. This is the most useful of all the lasso tools, suitable for creating complex selections where there is a defined outline—for example, isolating a figure from a plain background.

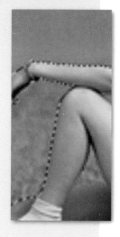

Virtual makeup bag

Along with the Clone Stamp and Brush tools, this group of tools make up what Nurse J. Peg likes to think of as her virtual makeup bag. Invaluable to any image retoucher—especially those in the fashion and beauty industries—they are ideal for many cosmetic applications, including removing fine lines, concealing spots, and changing the color of lipstick.

The Healing Brush

The Healing Brush is an intelligent paintbrush, which covers up image imperfections by seamlessly merging them into the surrounding area. Like the Clone Stamp tool (which we'll meet on *page 16*), the Healing Brush samples pixels from one part of an image. Holding the **Alt/⌥** key and clicking sets a sample source point, which is used to paint over imperfections in another part of the image. The Healing Brush separately measures the texture, color, and luminosity of the source point and then matches this information to that of the destination area, creating a perfect blend. With options to set the source point from a sampled section of the image or from a selected pattern, the Healing Brush is ideal for removing lines, wrinkles and blemishes to produce a flawless complexion.

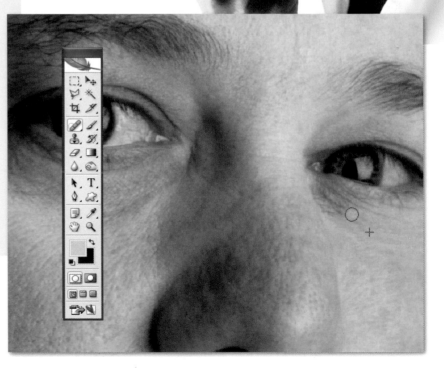

Patch tool

The Patch tool performs in much the same way as the Healing Brush, allowing you to repair a selected area of an image with pixels from another area of the image. Like the Healing Brush, the Patch tool also matches the texture, color, and luminosity of the sampled area to that of the destination area. The difference is in the tool's application. Instead of being used like a brush, the Patch tool creates a selection of the source area, which is then moved to the destination area. Selections can be made directly with the Patch tool, or by any of the selection tools before the Patch tool is employed. The selected area is then simply dragged to the destination area, and upon release of the mouse button, the patch is applied. The Patch tool has options to patch from source (select the damaged area and move to the good area), to patch from destination (select the good area and move to the damaged area), as well as the option to add a pattern to the selection.

Color Replacement tool

The Color Replacement tool provides a simplified solution to the problem of replacing a specific color within an image. There are other Photoshop tools that may perform this task better, but none are as easy to use. For certain procedures, such as removing red eye from images taken with direct flash, the Color Replacement tool is just what the doctor ordered. Using the Color Replacement tool is simply a case of painting over the unwanted color in an image with that of your own chosen foreground color. There are various tool options to adjust, including the sampling options: select Once for the color replacement to be based on the first point clicked on; only that color and shades of that color within the specified tolerance will be replaced. If the Continuous option is selected, the sample point is constantly updated as you move the tool across the image, replacing the sample point color with that of the selected foreground color.

The foundation tools

SHORTCUT   Hit the **S** key to select the Clone Stamp tool, or hold down the **SHIFT** key while repeatedly pressing the **S** key, to toggle between the Clone Stamp and Pattern Stamp versions of the tool.

This is another collection of tools essential in any cosmetic retouching work. They may not be as intelligent or as exciting to use as the Healing Brush or Patch tool, but do not undervalue them as basic Photoshop tools. Nurse J. Peg views them as the foundation in her virtual makeup bag, making them indispensable to any Photoshop cosmetic surgeon.

Clone Stamp tool

At first glance, the Clone Stamp may appear to be a simpler version of the Healing Brush, but in practice it is actually far more useful. Not merely restricted to performing retouching and general repair jobs, the Clone Stamp can be used to perfectly duplicate any specific portion of an image. Check the Aligned option box to define a constant relationship between the source and destination points, then select a sample source point by holding down the **Alt/⌥** key and clicking with the mouse. Move the cursor over to the destination point and then paint with the mouse to replicate the source area. The source point can even be selected from a separate image, giving you the option to add elements from other images without copying and pasting. Checking the Use All Layers option box allows you to source and copy selected sample data from a composite image. The Pattern Stamp version of the tool lets you choose any of the preset patterns from the Tool Options bar as a source point, while checking the Impressionist option adds a soft, haphazard jitter to the pattern.

SHORTCUT   Hit the **B** key to select the Brush tool or the **F5** key to open up the Brushes palette.

Brush tool

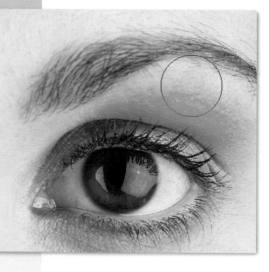

The Brush tool is a common feature present in all image-editing programs. It allows you to paint onto an image with the selected foreground color and is perfect for applying makeup effects to portraits. There are a large number of preset brushes to choose from, and any brush size can be selected from 1 pixel up to a maximum of 2500 pixels in diameter. The hardness of the brush can be adjusted, along with the brush's opacity and flow rate. The airbrush mode reproduces the effects of that tool—if you hold the mouse in one position, paint will build up and spread outward across the canvas. If you keep the mouse moving, it is applied evenly. To customize a brush even further, open the Brushes palette by pressing the **F5** key or by clicking on the Brushes palette tab at the far right of the options bar. From here extra options can be found, such as the Wet Edge option. This builds up density at the edges of the brush strokes, imitating the effect of painting with watercolor paints. Grouped with the Brush tool is the Pencil tool, which produces a hard-edged line more suited to drawing than retouching.

SHORTCUT   Hit the **Y** key to select the History Brush tool.

History Brush tool

The History Brush allows you to paint back details from a previous image state, or Snapshot, into the present image state. This is great for making selected areas of an image look like they did before adjustments were made to the whole image—for example, quickly reinstating brightly colored eyes after reducing the saturation of the whole image. To use the History Brush tool, first select it from the Toolbox, then go to the History palette and click on the left column of the previous state or Snapshot you wish to paint back from. Return to the image and paint over the areas you would like to return to that selected previous state. Grouped with the History Brush is the Art History Brush. In common with the History Brush, this tool allows you to use the source data from a previous state or Snapshot, but uses abstract, stylized painting strokes to replicate different artistic styles.

Erase, blur, sharpen & smudge

With the exception of from the Eraser, this selection of tools is not the most important to the aspiring Photoshop surgeon. Used sparingly, however, at the right time and in the right situation, they can produce remarkable results.

SHORTCUT *Hit the **E** key to select the Eraser tool, or hold down the **ALT/⌥** key as you paint to erase to the currently selected history state.*

ERASER TOOLS

Eraser

The Eraser tool is available in three sub-tools. The first and most useful is the standard Eraser, which makes the pixels of an image layer transparent, allowing the underlying layer to show through. If used on the background layer, the pixels are erased to "reveal" the background color. If the Erase to History option is selected in the Tool Options bar, the Eraser behaves like the History Brush, erasing pixels to reveal a previous state.

Background Eraser

The second Eraser is the Background Eraser, which allows you to erase the background of an image while maintaining the edges of an object in the foreground. It works by sampling the color at the center of the brush and deletes that color wherever it appears inside the brush. In other words, if you go over the edges of an object that is a different color than that you have chosen it doesn't matter, as only the sampled colors (within the set tolerances) will be erased.

Magic Eraser

The final variant is the Magic Eraser. This acts in a similar way to the Magic Wand tool—click on an area you wish to remove, and the Magic Eraser removes all the neighboring pixels with the same color values. Uncheck the Contiguous box in the Tool Options bar and all the image pixels with matching color values (or within tolerances) will be erased.

SHORTCUT Hit the **R** key to select the Blur tool, or hold down the **SHIFT** key while repeatedly pressing the **R** key to scroll between the Blur, Sharpen, and Smudge tools.

Blur tool

The Blur tool is useful for softening selected areas of an image; it reacts like using the Gaussian Blur filter to selectively paint over the image, reducing detail and softening objects. The tool is perfect for reducing fine lines and wrinkles.

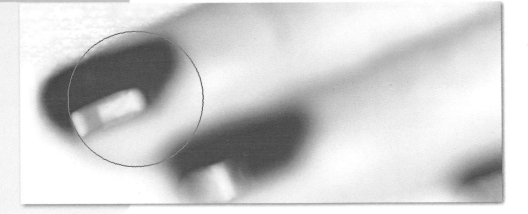

Sharpen tool

As you may have guessed, the Sharpen tool works in much the same way as the Blur tool, but sharpens selected areas of the image instead of blurring them. I tend to steer clear of this tool, as oversharpening can produce a jagged, pixelated appearance. I much prefer to create a feather-edged selection of the area and gradually apply the Unsharp Mask filter until the correct amount of sharpening is achieved.

SHORTCUT Hold down the **ALT/⌥** key when painting with the Smudge tool to temporarily change to the Finger Painting option. Release the **ALT/⌥** key to turn the Finger Painting option off.

Smudge tool

The Smudge tool credibly simulates the action of smudging wet paint with your fingertip. It works by selecting the color of the pixels where the tool is first clicked, and "pushing" them in the direction in which the tool is moved. The Tool Options bar allows you to select the Blend Mode and the Strength of the tool, as well as giving you the option to Use All Layers. This allows you to smudge colors from all the visible layers. The Finger Painting option uses the currently selected foreground color as the start point.

The darkroom tools

This group of tools is designed to replicate traditional photographic darkroom techniques for regulating the exposure of a print to light in order to lighten (dodge) or darken (burn) specific areas of the image.

SHORTCUT *Hit the **O** key to select the Dodge tool, or hold down the **Shift** key while repeatedly pressing the **O** key to scroll between the Dodge, Blur, and Sponge tools. Alternatively, hold down the **ALT/⌥** key when using the Dodge tool to temporarily switch to the Burn tool.*

Dodge tool

Traditionally the dodge tool is a black card used by a photographer during the darkroom printing process. The card is placed between the light source and the photographic paper to reduce the paper's exposure to light in specific areas. The Photoshop version of the Dodge tool performs much the same task, but with far greater control over the end result. The exposure setting of the tool can be adjusted, allowing you to alter the strength of the dodging effect, along with the option to use the tool selectively on shadows, midtones, or highlights—for example, you can lighten midtones without affecting the adjacent shadows or highlights. The Dodge tool is great when used at low exposure for gently lightening dark areas around the eyes.

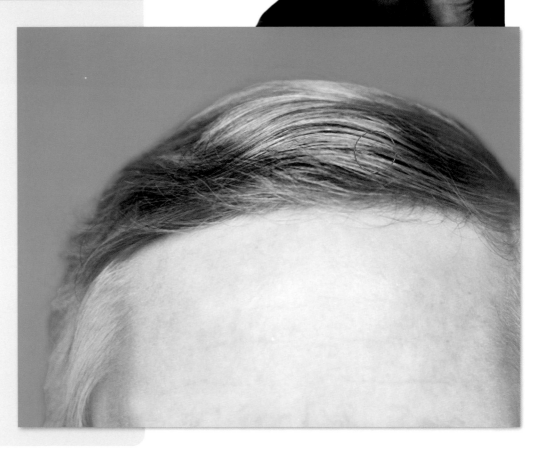

Burn tool

Producing the opposite effect to the Dodge tool, the Burn tool darkens selective parts of an image, imitating the technique of burning. This is where a photographer would use his hand to form an O shape, or a black card with a hole in it, and use it to expose certain areas of the print to extra light (thereby darkening that area of the print). Like the Dodge tool, the exposure of the tool can be adjusted, along with the option to use the tool on shadows, midtones, or highlights. The Burn tool is very useful for creating shadows to help define muscle mass.

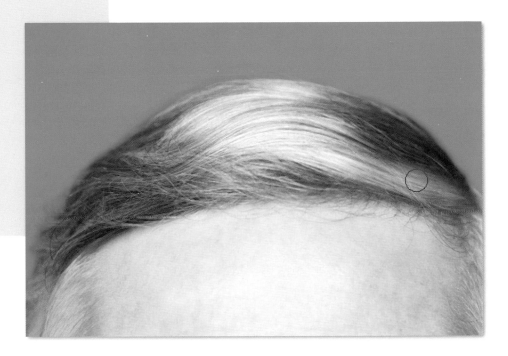

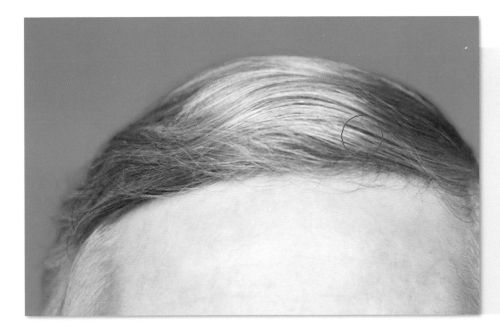

Sponge tool

The Sponge tool subtly changes the localized saturation of an image. It can be used on color images to increase or decrease saturation, while in grayscale mode the tool increases or decreases contrast by moving gray levels away from or toward middle gray. Used sparingly, the Sponge tool can be useful for small jobs such as boosting the saturation of lip color.

Shape drawing tools

Photoshop contains a comprehensive collection of vector drawing tools that can be used to create and edit complex paths, which can then be turned into selections. It may take a little time to master the control of the Path tools, but persevere and you will soon realize why this group of tools is a crucial component of the Photoshop surgeon's tool kit.

SHORTCUT Hit the **P** key to select the Pen tool, or hold down the Shift key while repeatedly pressing the **P** key to toggle between the Pen and Freeform Pen tools. Alternatively, holding down the **Shift** key while using the Pen tool constrains the tool to creating angles of 45°.

PEN TOOLS

Pen tool

There are a number of variations available to the Pen Tool. The first is the mighty Pen itself, which is used to draw straight lines and smooth curves with great precision. To create a path, first choose the Paths option from the left side of the Tool Options bar; this is important, as the Pen tool automatically opens with the Shape Layers option selected. Position the pointer where you want to draw, and click to define the first anchor point. Reposition the mouse, adding anchor points by clicking again—these points are automatically joined to form a path. To create a curve, click and drag the mouse in the direction you wish the path to follow. Two handles will appear from the anchor point; the direction and length of these handles define the shape of the curve. Click on the original anchor point to complete the path shape, or click on any unwanted anchor points to remove them. If you would like a preview of the path's direction before adding anchor points, select the Rubber Band option from the drop-down sub-menu in the Tool Options bar.

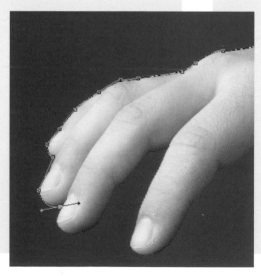

Freeform Pen tool

The Freeform Pen tool performs much like the Lasso tool, creating a path wherever you draw and—if you are good at drawing—offering a very accurate way of creating shapes. Anchor points are added to the path, which can be edited later when the path is completed.

Anchor Point tools

The Add Anchor Point and Delete Anchor Point tools do exactly what their respective titles suggest—either adding anchor points to, or deleting anchor points from, an existing path.

Convert Point tool

The Convert Point tool enables you to convert corner anchor points into smooth anchor points by clicking and dragging to generate handles, or smooth anchor points into corner anchor points by simply clicking on the appropriate anchor point.

SELECTION TOOLS

Path Selection tool

Direct Selection tool

The Path Selection tool is used for selecting, moving, copying, deleting, and combining paths or filled shape layers within an image. The Direct Selection Tool is used for selecting specific path anchor points in order to reshape the path.

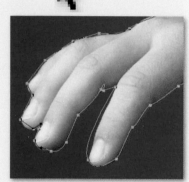

SHAPE TOOLS

The shape tools enable you to create pre-defined, editable shapes such as Rectangle, Rounded Rectangle, Ellipse, Polygon, Line, and Custom Shape in three separate forms.

Shape layer

Creates a layer mask that contains two components: the shape, which defines the boundary of the mask, and a fill, which appears within the shape. Once created, the shape may be modified with the Pen and Path Selection tools.

Paths

Creates a path outline that is independent of the current layer. You can stroke or fill the path, but the path always remains separate from the added pixels. If you move the path, the stroke or fill stays where it is, allowing you to stroke or fill the same path over and over in different locations. Like Shape layers, Paths are vector based, which allows them to be transformed, resized, and modified without quality degradation.

Fill pixels

Adds a shape filled with pixels to the current layer. It is advisable to create new shapes on separate layers, so create one before using this tool. This allows the shape to be more easily modified and moved without disturbing the other elements in the image.

Each shape tool has a selection of specific options, which vary for each shape. For example, you can set options that allow you to draw a rectangle with fixed dimensions, or a line with arrowheads added to either or both ends. These options can be accessed from the drop-down menu in the Tool Options bar.

Although shapes are not the most relevant topic in a book on photo retouching, it is surprising how flexible they can be— check out the example on *page 62*, showing how they are used in the application of a tattoo.

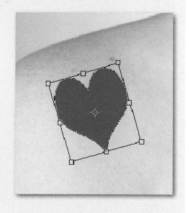

Liquify command

The Liquify filter is an extremely powerful tool that enables you to push, pull, rotate, reflect, pucker, or bloat any selected area of an active image. Essential to any creative Photoshop surgeon, the Liquify tool applies distortions that can be as subtle or as extreme as required, and can suit almost any surgical situation. Ideal for creating digital liposuction effects, you will be amazed at the results obtained by this particularly useful tool.

To use the Liquify filter, we must first open the Liquify dialog box—this can be found in the drop-down **Filter >** menu or by using the keyboard shortcut **Ctrl/⌘+Shift+X**. Once opened, you will see that the dialog box contains three main areas. Let's examine these more closely…

LIQUIFY INTERFACE

Toolbar

The Toolbar runs down the left edge of the dialog box and contains a variety of tools, all of which may be used on the image in the preview window.

Preview window

This is where an editable preview of the active image opens up.

Options palette

From here, various options can be applied to the tools, masks, and transformations made to an image in the preview window.

LIQUIFY OPTIONS

There are a number of options that can be applied to the tools in the Liquify dialog box. These include options to adjust the brush size, brush density, brush pressure, brush rate, and turbulent jitter. There are also options to adjust the mode in which the image is reconstructed after distortions have been made, along with various mask options. Another useful function is the Show Mesh option, which adds a grid to the image, enabling you to easily identify where distortions have been applied. Meshes can even be saved and applied to other images to create the same distortions on different photos.

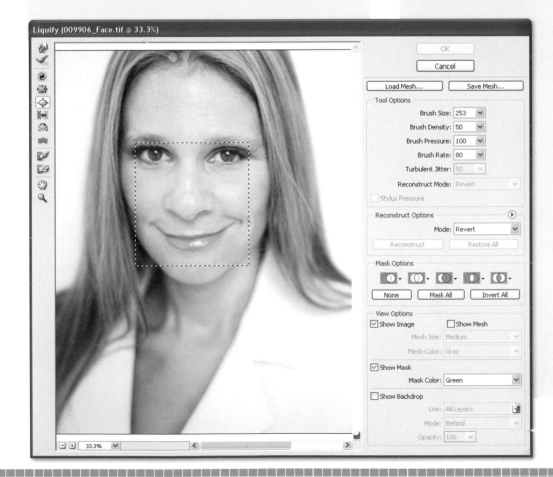

LIQUIFY TOOLS

Warp Forward

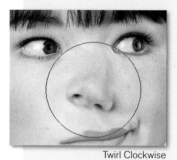

Twirl Clockwise

Pucker

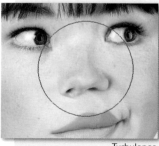

Turbulence

Forward Warp tool
 Hold down the mouse button and move the mouse to push pixels in that direction. **(W)**

Reconstruct tool
 This tool allows you to selectively reconstruct areas of an image that have previously been distorted. **(R)**

Twirl Clockwise tool
 This tool twirls the image pixels clockwise when the mouse button is held (or counter-clockwise if the **Alt/⌥** key is held too). **(C)**

Pucker tool
 Hold down the mouse button or drag to shrink pixels toward the center of the selected brush area. **(S)**

Bloat tool
 Hold down the mouse button or drag to magnify pixels away from the center of the selected brush area. **(B)**

Push Left tool
 Moves pixels to the left when you drag the tool straight up, and moves pixels to the right when you drag it down. **(O)**

Mirror tool
 Drag the mouse to reflect the area at right angles to the direction of the stroke. **(M)**

Turbulence tool
 This produces random turbulent distortions and is ideal for cloud or wave effects. **(T)**

Freeze tool
Hold down the mouse button and drag to freeze specific areas of an image, protecting them from distortion. **(F)**

Thaw tool
Hold down the mouse button and drag to thaw selective areas of a frozen image to allow these areas to be distorted. **(D)**

Hand tool
This lets you drag the image around the preview window. Hold down **Space** when using any other tool for the same effect.

Zoom tool
Click and drag to zoom in to a specific area of an image, or hold down the **Alt/⌥** key and click to zoom out.

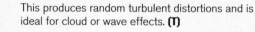

Extract command

The Extract filter provides a sophisticated method of isolating foreground objects from their backgrounds. This tool is so clever that even images with intricate edges, such as wispy hair, can easily be extracted from their backgrounds with the minimum of effort. Simply draw around the object you want to extract with the Highlighter tool, making sure you completely surround the object, then use the Fill tool to apply a mask to the object before pressing the Preview button. The Extract filter automatically detects the edges of the object and removes the background; the cleanup tools can then be used to tidy up the edges of the extraction in the preview window before the results are applied.

Like the Liquify filter, the Extract filter can be found in the drop-down **Filter >** menu and has the same three distinct areas.

EXTRACT INTERFACE

Toolbar

The Toolbar contains a variety of tools, which may all be used on the image in the preview window.

Preview window

This is where an editable preview of the active image opens up.

Options palette

From here, various options can be applied to the tools.

EXTRACT OPTIONS

There are a number of options that can be applied to the tools in the Extract dialog box. These include options for selecting the Highlight brush size and color, and the Fill color. There is also an option to select Smart Highlighting. This works like the Magnetic Lasso and automatically detects an object's edge as you draw around it. Smart Highlighting can be temporarily disabled by holding down the **Ctrl/⌘** key as you drag the mouse. Extraction options include the Forced Foreground option, and a Texture option that, when selected, allows an object to be extracted based on texture content as well as color.

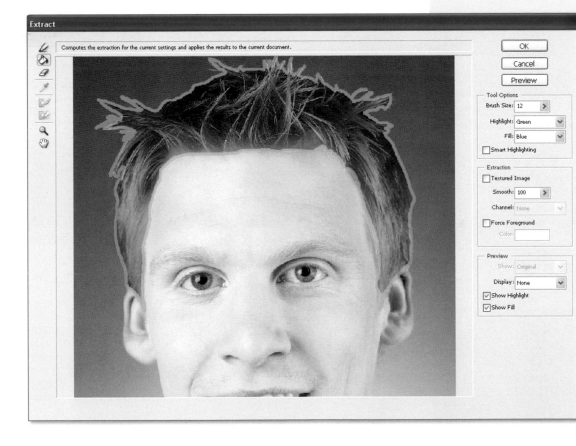

EXTRACT TOOLS

Highlighter tool

Hold down the mouse button and drag the mouse to draw around the object that requires isolating, ensuring the highlight slightly overlaps both the foreground object and its background.

Fill tool

Click inside the highlighted object to apply a mask to the object (clicking a masked area with the Fill tool removes the fill).

Eraser tool

Hold down the mouse button and drag over the highlight to erase it, or press **Alt/⌥+Backspace/←** to remove the entire highlight.

Eyedropper tool

Used only when the Forced Foreground option is selected, you need to click inside the object in order to select a sample foreground color.

Cleanup tool

After previewing, use this tool around the extracted edge of the object to remove unwanted background artifacts and fill gaps in the object.

Touchup tool

The Touchup tool is also used after previewing, this time to go around the extracted edge of the object to sharpen it (done by removing opacity from the background and adding opacity to the object).

Zoom tool

Click and drag to zoom in to a specific area of an image, or hold down the **Alt/⌥** key and click to zoom out.

Hand tool

This lets you drag the image around the preview window. Hold **Space** when using any other tool to temporarily select the Hand tool.

Quick Mask mode & Alpha channels

Masks are a fundamental requirement for any Photoshop surgeon; they protect selected areas of an image, allowing you to apply color adjustments, filters, or other effects to the remainder of the image without affecting the masked area. Masks can be created within Photoshop in a number of ways, but without doubt the simplest is the Quick Mask mode. A mask can be created entirely in Quick Mask mode, or started from any selection, which can then be edited in Quick Mask mode. Masks can be saved as alpha channels, allowing them to be used again on the same image (or even on a different one).

Creating a Quick Mask

For this simple demonstration we will use the Quick Mask mode to create a mask over this woman, so that we can blur the background without affecting her. This will give the impression of a narrow depth of field, focusing attention onto the subject and away from the background.

Before

1 First, use the Rectangular marquee tool to make a very quick and rough selection of the woman. Now, invert the selection by clicking on Inverse in the drop-down **Select >** menu (or by using the keyboard shortcut **Ctrl/⌘+Shift+I**). This will switch the selection from the woman to the background.

2 Enter the Quick Mask mode by clicking on the Quick Mask mode button in the toolbox, or by hitting the **Q** key. This adds a red-colored overlay mask to the area outside of the selection.

Alpha channels

Alpha channels are separate grayscale channels created to save selections independently from the RGB or CMYK channels that make up the image itself. When a selection is saved as an alpha channel, it is stored at the bottom of the Channels palette, from where it can be recalled and applied to the image at any time.

3 As you can see, the mask not only covers the woman, but also parts of the background. We can now use the paintbrush to edit the mask; painting with white removes the mask, while painting with black adds to it. Using a soft-edged brush, paint around the hair. The soft-edged brush acts to give the mask itself a soft edge.

A temporary mask can be converted to a permanent alpha channel by switching to standard mode and choosing **Save Selection** from the **Select** menu. The selection can then be saved as a new channel or added to, subtracted from, or intersected with an existing channel.

Alpha channels can be edited with the painting tools as masks—paint black to add to the channel or use white to subtract from it.

4 With the mask complete, press **Q** (or click the Standard Mode button in the Toolbox) to return to the original image. A selection border now surrounds the unprotected area of the Quick Mask. From the **Filter >** menu, choose **Gaussian Blur** and enter a radius of 12 pixels. Click OK to apply the blur to the background.

After

Layers, Layer masks & Adjustment layers

Layers are of paramount importance to any creative Photoshop user. They permit enormously complex composite images to be created in very little time and with the minimum of effort. Imagine layers of transparent acetate stacked on top of a background image, each individual sheet containing a fragment of another image. When viewed together the layers create a composite image that can be infinitely adjusted. Layers can be added, removed, transformed, color corrected, and blended together using layer masks and blend modes. They can have any number of filters and effects applied to them, or they can be grouped together, allowing the manipulation of multiple layers as a single object.

Creating a layer mask

I thought it might be fun to demonstrate the results of applying a layer mask by performing a simple gender-switch operation on this image of a girl looking into a mirror.

Before

Layer masks

If layers are the lifeblood of Photoshop, then layer masks should be seen as a blood transfusion. They allow separate images to be seamlessly blended together by controlling the amount and opacity of each layer present in the overall image. Once added to a layer, layer masks can be edited over and over again without permanently affecting the pixels of the layer. They only need to be permanently applied to the layer when you are completely satisfied with the results.

1 First I placed a portrait image of a young man on top of the girl looking into the mirror. I then lowered the opacity of the top layer to 50% and selected **Free Transform** from the drop-down **Edit** menu (**Ctrl/⌘+T**). I then repositioned the young man's head so that his eyes were over those of the girl, and double-clicked the mouse to apply the transformation.

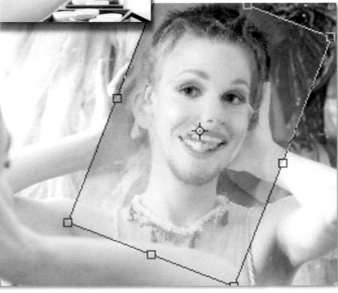

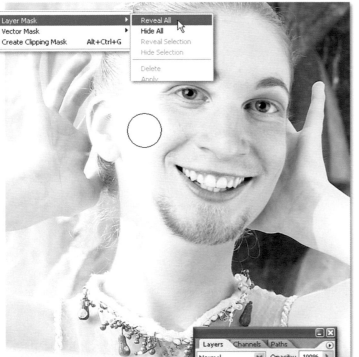

Adjustment layers

Adjustment layers provide the opportunity to experiment on an image with various color and tonal adjustments without permanently affecting the pixels contained within. To create a new adjustment layer, just click on the New Adjustment Layer button at the bottom of the Layers palette. A drop-down menu will appear, offering a number of options such as Color Balance, Brightness/Contrast, and Hue/Saturation. Once a selection has been made, the relevant dialog box or command appears, allowing the selected modification to be made to the adjustment layer. To apply the results of an adjustment layer permanently, select one of the merge options from the bottom of the Layers menu.

It is important to bear in mind that an adjustment layer doesn't just affect the layer immediately below it, but all of its underlying layers.

2 I then selected **Layer > Add Layer Mask > Reveal All** and used a soft-edged black brush to remove the unwanted areas of the top layer to reveal the layer underneath. If you remove too much of the layer, simply paint with white to reveal the top layer.

3 When I was happy with the adjustments made to the layer mask, I Right/Control-clicked on the trash can at the bottom of the layers palette, and selected Apply from the pop-up dialog box to apply the results of the mask to the layer.

4 I then pressed **Ctrl/⌘+B** to open the Color Balance dialog box, and added more yellow to the midtones of the portrait layer in order to blend it with the color cast of the background layer. Finally the layers were merged, revealing the slightly disturbing image of what appears to be a young lady with a beard looking into a mirror.

After

BLENDING MODES
A visual guide

Aside from layer masks, you can combine different images in all sorts of ways using Photoshop's comprehensive range of blending modes. These can be accessed via the drop-down menu at the top of the Layers palette, and produce a wide range of visual effects. When a blending mode is applied to a layer, it controls how the pixels in the layer affect those of the underlying layer.

To demonstrate this, the following pages contain illustrations showing the effects created by each of the blending modes on the same two pictures. Where possible I have kept the opacity of the top layer set to 100%, though in some cases it was necessary to reduce the opacity of the top layer (the woman) in order to clearly illustrate the effect achieved.

Normal (75% opacity)

This is the default mode. With the opacity set at 100%, the underlying layer cannot be seen. Lowering the opacity of the blend layer reduces the pixel intensity by averaging the value of its color pixels with those of the underlying layer, allowing the underlying image to show through.

Dissolve (60% opacity)

As with Normal mode, no change can be seen with the opacity set at 100%, but when the opacity of the blend layer is lowered, it merges with the underlying layer via a randomly diffused pattern of pixels. These pixels become increasingly visible as the blend layer opacity is reduced.

Darken (100% opacity)

Darken mode views the color information in both the blend layer and the underlying layer; it then selects whichever is the darker as the resulting color. Lighter pixels are replaced, while darker pixels remain unchanged.

Multiply (100% opacity)

Multiply mode also looks at the color information of each layer, but this time it multiplies the base color with the blend color, resulting in a darker image (unless any areas of the blend layer are white, in which case the base color is left unchanged).

Color Burn (100% opacity)

Color Burn mode views the color information in each layer and blends the darker colors of the blend layer with the base layer by increasing the contrast. Blending with white has no effect on the image.

Linear Burn (100% opacity)

Linear Burn mode produces an effect similar to Darken or Multiply, only darker. It does this by darkening the base color to reflect the blend color by decreasing its brightness. Blending with white has no overall effect on the image.

Lighten (100% opacity)

Lighten mode views the color information in both the blend layer and the underlying layer; it then selects whichever is the lighter as the resulting color. Pixels darker than the base color are replaced, while lighter pixels remain the same.

Screen (100% opacity)

Screen mode views the color information in each layer and multiplies the opposites of the base and blend layer colors, resulting in a lighter color (apart from any areas of the blend layer that are black, which remain unchanged).

Color Dodge (90% opacity)

Color Dodge mode produces the opposite effect to Color Burn mode by viewing the color information in each layer and then brightening the base color to reflect the blend color by decreasing its contrast. Blending with black has no effect on the image.

Linear Dodge (100% opacity)

Linear Dodge mode produces the opposite effect to Linear Burn mode by viewing the color information in each layer and then brightening the base color to reflect the blend color (increasing its brightness). Blending with black has no effect on the image.

Overlay (100% opacity)

Overlay mode superimposes the blend layer over the base layer, multiplying or concealing colors depending on the color values of the base layer. The base layer color is mixed with, as opposed to replaced by, the blend layer color, but retains its shadows and highlights.

Soft Light (100% opacity)

Soft Light mode produces a similar but more subtle effect to that of Overlay mode. If the blend color is darker than 50% gray, the entire image will darken. If it is lighter than 50% gray, the entire image will lighten, mimicking the effect of shining a diffused spotlight on the image.

Hard Light (100% opacity)

Soft Light mode produces a similar but more distinct effect to that of Overlay mode. If the blend color is darker than 50% gray, the entire image is darkened (as if using the Multiply mode). If it is lighter than 50% gray, the entire image will lighten as if using Screen. The resulting effect is like shining a harsh spotlight on the image.

Vivid Light (100% opacity)

Vivid Light mode burns or dodges the colors by increasing or decreasing contrast. If the blend color is darker than 50% gray, the entire image is darkened by increasing contrast. If it is lighter than 50% gray, the entire image is lightened by decreasing contrast. The resulting effect is like Hard Light mode, only stronger.

Linear Light (100% opacity)

Linear Light mode burns or dodges the colors by decreasing or increasing brightness. If the blend color is darker than 50% gray, the image is made darker by decreasing brightness. If it is lighter than 50% gray, the image is made lighter by increasing brightness. The resulting effect is like Vivid Light mode, only stronger.

Pin Light (100% opacity)

Pin Light mode produces an effect similar to Soft Light, but more pronounced, by replacing colors depending on the blend color. If the blend color is lighter than 50% gray, pixels darker than the blend color are replaced, while pixels lighter than the blend color stay the same. If the blend color is darker than 50%, pixels lighter than the blend color are replaced and darker ones remain unchanged.

Hard Mix (100% opacity)

Hard Mix mode produces a poster-like image containing up to eight colors; it is made up from a mix of the base color and the luminosity of the blend layer.

Difference (100% opacity)

Difference mode views the color information in both the blend layer and the underlying layer, and subtracts either the blend color from the base color or the base color from the blend color, depending on which has the greater brightness value.

Exclusion (100% opacity)

Exclusion mode produces a similar but more muted version of Difference mode. Blending with white inverts the base color values, while blending with black has no effect.

Hue (100% opacity)

Hue mode produces a new color by combining the hue of the blend color with the luminance and saturation of the base color.

Saturation (100% opacity)

Saturation mode produces a new color by combining the saturation of the blend color with the luminance and hue of the base color.

Color (100% opacity)

Color mode produces a new color by combining the hue and saturation of the blend color with the luminance of the base color.

Luminosity (100% opacity)

Luminosity mode produces a new color by combining the luminance of the blend color with the hue and saturation of the base color. The resulting effect is the opposite of Color mode.

CONTENTS

SECTION 2

Supermodel looks

Meet Dr. Jackson's able assistant Nurse J. Peg as she guides you through the retouching techniques used on movie stars, pop icons, and magazine cover models

FACE TO FACE
Perfect symmetry

Before

Dear Nurse J. Peg,
My boyfriend told me that nobody has a perfectly symmetrical face, but I don't know whether to believe him or not. He is always playing tricks on me. I have scrutinized models' faces in magazines and I'm sure that some of them looked perfectly symmetrical. I told him that you would know, and if I found out that he was lying to me again I would finish with him. So could you please settle this silly dispute, for the sake of our relationship.
Yours faithfully,
Tracy

Nurse J. Peg says...

Dear Tracy,

I'm afraid your boyfriend is telling the truth—faces are not perfectly symmetrical, but they are often manipulated that way in order to make a model seem more beautiful or striking. This is a simple procedure—it can be completed in a matter of minutes. So why not try my formula for perfect symmetry? Then perhaps you should apologize to your boyfriend for calling him a liar.

Regards,
Nurse J. Peg

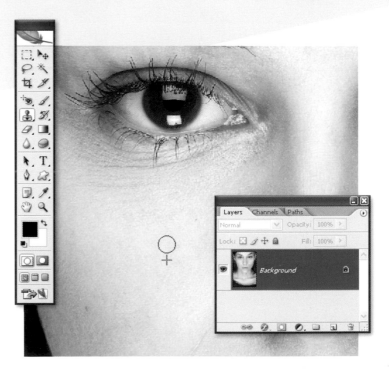

1 To make the most of this technique for creating perfect facial symmetry, your image should be taken face-on, and under even lighting conditions, as it is best if shadows are kept to a minimum. Start by opening the image in Photoshop and then decide which half of the face to duplicate. For this example I chose the left side, as I found it the more attractive side of the face. First, remove any blemishes. Select the Clone Stamp tool from the Tools palette by pressing the **(S)** key. Hold down the **Alt/⌥** key as you click with the mouse on a clean section of skin to create a sample point. This should be an area of nearby, similarly lit, but unblemished skin. Now clone the sampled skin over any minor spots and blemishes on the left side of the face only.

2 Next press the **(M)** key to select the Rectangular Marquee tool and drag out a rectangular selection across the left side of the face so that the right edge of the selection border runs straight down the center of the nose. Right/control-click within the selection and choose the **Layer via Copy** option from the pop-up menu. Now go to **Edit > Transform > Flip Horizontal** to flip over the copied selection, and then use the Move tool **(V)** to reposition it over the right side of the face. Use the right and left arrow keys to nudge the layer one pixel at a time, until no obvious join can be seen running down the nose.

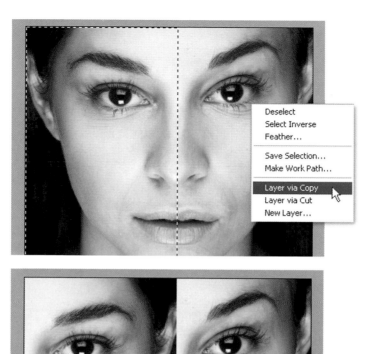

3 You now need to blend the edges of the copy layer with the original. To do this, use a layer mask. Go to **Layer > Add Layer Mask > Reveal All** or click on the Add Layer Mask icon near the bottom of the Toolbox. Press the **(B)** key to select the Brush tool, right/control-click on the image to open the brush picker dialog box, and choose a large soft-edged brush before clicking OK to close the dialog box.

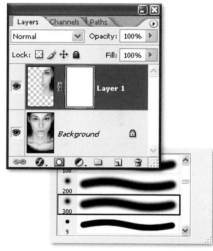

4 Paint over the edges of the layer with black to remove the mask around the neck and hair, letting the original layer below show through. Although you want to make the face symmetrical, you don't want to make it obvious; keeping all the original neck and hair fools the viewer into believing the image is genuine. Reduce the opacity of the brush to 70% and gently run down the join along the center of the face to remove any hard edges. If too much of the mask is removed, press the **(X)** key to switch the foreground to white, and paint the mask back in. Once you are happy with the results of the blending, press **Ctrl/⌘+E** to combine the layers and complete your perfectly symmetrical face.

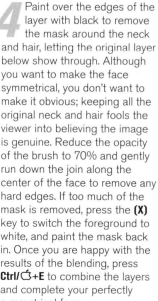

After

SMILING EYES

Make those brown eyes blue

Dear Jane,

I wonder if you could help me. I'm thinking of buying colored contact lenses but I'm really not sure which color to go for. A friend of mine wears them but I think she picked the wrong color because they just make her eyes look really weird. Is there any way you could show me which color would look best against my complexion and hair color? Ideally I would like them to look quite natural. I don't want to make the same mistake as my friend and end up looking like Marilyn Manson.

Many thanks,
Stacy

Nurse J. Peg says...

Dear Stacy,

No problem! Just recreate my effortless four-point formula for producing bright, beautiful, and colorful eyes, and forget all notions of looking like Marilyn Manson. In fact I would rather you thought of Crystal Gayle—after all, following this procedure could make your brown eyes blue.

Best wishes,
Jane

Before

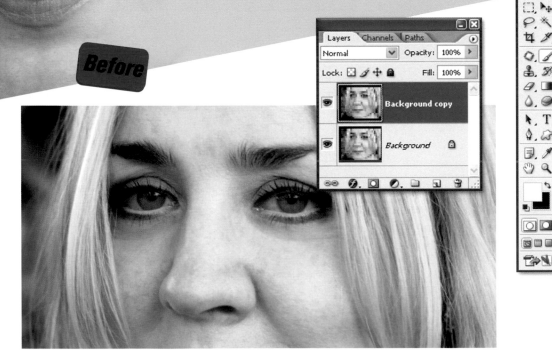

1 Before proceeding with any manipulation, first copy the image by selecting the Duplicate Layer option from the Layer Menu. Name the new layer in the Duplicate Layer dialog, and click OK. Any alterations now made to the image will be applied to the copy, leaving the original image unaffected. We will start by making the whites of the eyes whiter. To do this, first make a selection of the whites of the eyes by pressing **(Q)** to enter the Quick Mask mode, and paint over the white areas of the eye with a black paintbrush. If you accidentally paint over the iris, use a white brush to remove the mask.

2 Press the **(Q)** key again to enter standard mode and invert the selection by pressing **Ctrl/⌘+Shift+I** (or by selecting **Inverse** from the Select menu). Go to **Select > Feather**, or press **Alt/⌥+Ctrl/⌘+D** and enter a radius of 2 pixels in the dialog box. Click OK to apply. This will soften the edges of the selection, ensuring any adjustments made are not too obvious.

3 Go to **Image > Adjustments > Hue/Saturation** or press **Ctrl/⌘+U** to bring up the Hue/Saturation dialog box. Select Reds from the drop-down menu at the top of the dialog box and drag the Saturation slider to the left. This will reduce the bloodshot appearance of the eyes. Now select Master from the drop-down menu and drag the Lightness slider to the right to lighten the eyes. The amount of adjustment required will vary for each image, so you will need to experiment. Just remember that too much adjustment can produce an unnatural appearance.

4 When you are happy with the results, click OK to apply the changes, and then press **Ctrl/⌘+D** to deselect. We will now turn our attention to changing the color of the eyes. Repeat stages one and two to select the iris of each eye, and then press **Ctrl/⌘+B** or go to **Image > Adjustments > Color Balance** to bring up the Color Balance dialog box. By repositioning the color sliders we can now create any eye color we desire. In this example I made the eyes an intense and vibrant blue by increasing the amounts of blue and cyan in the midtones. When you are happy with the results, click OK to apply the changes and **Ctrl/⌘+D** to deselect.

LUSCIOUS LASHES
Creating longer eyelashes

Dear Jane,

I am obsessed with the '60s—I love the fashion, the music, the interior design, and everything. If I had to choose my favorite thing it would have to be the look created by models such as Twiggy and Jean Shrimpton. I absolutely adore the way they made their eyes so striking using pale makeup and false eyelashes. I like the look so much that I have been trying to recreate it on a photo of myself. I've had success adjusting the tone of the image, but I'm having real trouble trying to emphasize my eyelashes. Is there a procedure you could share with me?

Regards,
Susan

Nurse J. Peg says...

Dear Susan,

As you so rightly point out, the key to the '60s look was the way false eyelashes overemphasized the eyes. Recreating this effect in Photoshop is really quite simple, as you will see. To recreate the whole look in real life is a little more difficult, unless you look like a stick and weigh virtually nothing.

Regards,

Nurse J. Peg

Before

Rectangular Marquee Tool (M)

1 Use the Toolbox (or the shortcut **(M)** key) to select the Rectangular Marquee tool and make a simple rectangular selection surrounding the eye, before choosing **Select > Inverse** (or pressing **Shft+Ctrl/⌘+I**) to invert the selection. Now enter Quick Mask mode by pressing the **(Q)** key—a transparent red overlay will now fill the selection covering the eye.

2 Select the Brush tool by pressing **(B)** and paint over the mask with white to remove the areas over the eyelid and below the eyelashes. Do not remove the mask between the eyelashes. Hit **(Q)** again to return to standard mode, and invert the selection again by pressing **Shift+Ctrl/⌘+I** (or by choosing **Select > Inverse** from the menu).

3 Now that the eyelashes are roughly selected, copy the selection to a new layer by pressing **Ctrl/⌘+C** to copy the section and **Ctrl/⌘+V** to paste it to a new layer. Go to **Edit > Transform** and select Distort from the drop down sub-menu. You can now adjust the size of the copied eyelashes without affecting the original layer underneath.

After

4 Drag the bottom right and bottom left handles of the Transform bounding box out and down to create a trapezium. You will see this has the effect of lengthening and fanning out the eyelashes, without affecting the top of

the lashes where they meet the eyelid. The farther the bounding box handles are dragged, the longer the lashes will become, and the more they will resemble false lashes. When you're happy with the results, simply merge the layers together by hitting **Ctrl/⌘+E**.

Example 2

To fully illustrate the results that can be achieved using this technique, I have overemphasized the eyelashes on a closed-eye image. The same procedure works just as well on an open-eyed image, as can be seen in this more subtle example.

BETTER BROWS

Eyebrow trimming & shaping

Dear Nurse Peg,

I never realized just how cruel women could be. All my so-called friends have recently taken to calling me Groucho Marx when we are all out together just because I don't trim my eyebrows. I know they are only joking and don't realize the hurt they are causing, but I have gotten to the stage where if I don't do something about them (the eyebrows, that is) I will end up telling all my friends a few home truths. Could you show me any techniques to help me practice shaping my eyebrows before I do it for real?

Yours hopefully,
Danielle

Nurse J. Peg says...

"*Dear Danielle,*

Shaping eyebrows in Photoshop is quick and painless—just follow my simple technique. Plucking your own eyebrows may not be quite as enjoyable, but it should save you from the "wit" of your friends. If they still insist on calling you "Groucho" next time you're out, simply quote his line, "I've had a perfectly wonderful evening, but this wasn't it."

Regards,

Nurse J. Peg"

Before

1 Open the image you want to work on and then hit the **(Q)** key to enter Quick Mask mode. Press the **(B)** key to select the Brush tool, then press the **(D)** key to ensure the default black and white foreground and background colors are selected. Paint with black over the left eyebrow in the shape you wish to keep. As we are in Quick Mask mode, the painted area will appear as a red, semitransparent mask. To remove any part of the mask, press the **(X)** key to switch the foreground color to white and then paint over the areas of the mask you want to remove.

2 Repeat the painting process over the right eyebrow, taking care to match the shape with that of the left eyebrow. Now press the **(Q)** key again to exit Quick Mask mode and return to Standard mode. You will see that the areas around the masked eyebrows have now been turned into selections. Go to **Select > Feather** or press **Alt/⌥+Ctrl/⌘+D** to bring up the Feather Selection dialog box. Enter a value of 4 pixels, and press OK to apply the feather.

3 Select the Clone Stamp tool by pressing the **(S)** key, and choose a soft-edged brush from the tool options bar. Hold down the **Alt/⌥** key and click on a clean area of skin below the eyebrow to select a sample point. Now clone the skin over the eyebrows. Don't worry about going over the masked area of the eyebrows with the Clone Stamp tool, as only the area within the selection will be altered.

After

4 Once all the unwanted sections of eyebrow have been removed, press **Ctrl/⌘+D** to deselect. At this point you may be happy with the eyebrow trim results and not wish to go any farther, but if you would like to add a little bit more realism to the eyebrows, press **(R)** to select the Smudge tool from the Toolbox, then set the brush size to 2 pixels and the opacity to 95%. Now click and drag out single hairs around the eyebrow, always going in the same direction as the hairs, to complete the reshape.

DIGITAL LIPSTICK
Making color choice easy

Dear Nurse J. Peg,

Could you please show me a quick way of changing lipstick color in Photoshop? I have been using the Color Replacement tool to paint over the lips with a different color, but I find this very time consuming, especially if I'm not sure which color to use and need to experiment. I assume there must be a quicker way. Please can you help?

David

Nurse J. Peg says...

Dear David,

You're right! There are much quicker ways of altering lipstick color. The method I prefer also has the benefit of not affecting the original image, allowing you to experiment with many shades before making your final selection. So, to save time, just follow my simple three-step procedure for producing perfect lip color in a flash.

Regards,
Nurse J. Peg

Before

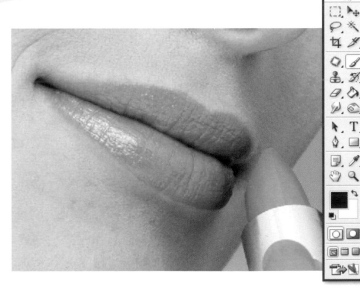

1 Start by hitting the **(Q)** key to enter Quick Mask mode. There are also mask toggle buttons near the bottom of the Toolbox, which look like two circles contained within two side-by-side rectangles. The right rectangle enters Quick Mask mode.

2 Use a soft-edged Brush **(B)** to paint a red transparent mask over the lips, then use the Eraser tool **(E)** to remove any excess areas of mask. Click on the left rectangle (or press the **(Q)** key again) to turn the area around the mask into a selection. From the **Select** menu, choose **Inverse** to invert the selection, then press **Ctrl/⌘+C** to copy the selection, and **Ctrl/⌘+V** to paste the selection to a new layer.

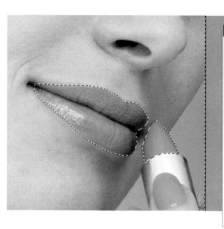

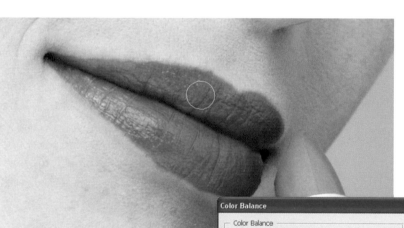

3 Press **Ctrl/⌘+B** to open the Color Balance dialog box. From here you can separately adjust the shadows, midtones, and highlight color sliders to create any shade of lipstick imaginable without affecting the original image. When you feel you have achieved the correct shade of lip color, simply press **Ctrl/⌘+E** to merge the two layers.

After

LIP SERVICE
Pain-free collagen injections

Dear Jane,

I'm an aspiring actress and my agent has lined up an audition with a top movie director. I am trying for the part of a gangster's moll who's seduced by Brad Pitt. This could be my big break, so I really don't want to mess it up, and would do anything to get it. My only worry is my lips; they are quite thin, and I was wondering how they'd look if I had collagen injections to plump them up a little. Ideally I would like them to look more seductive and kissable, since there is a lot of kissing in the part.

Yours sincerely,
Emma

Nurse J. Peg says...

Dear Emma,

The part sounds wonderful and I'm sure more kissable lips would be a great help in getting it. My only concern is that if you have too much collagen injected you may look like you've been slapped by Brad rather than seduced by him. I suggest you follow my example and show the results to your doctor as a guide.

Regards, Jane

P.S. Is there also a part in the film for a nurse who is seduced by Brad? Let me know.

Before

1 As the top lip is thinner than the bottom lip, we will start by making it a little larger so that it better matches the lower one. Select the Lasso tool by pressing the **(L)** key or by clicking on the Lasso icon in the Toolbox. Use the Lasso tool to draw a rough selection around the lips of the girl, then press **Ctrl/⌘+J** to copy the lips to a new layer.

2 Now open the Liquify dialog interface by pressing **Ctrl/⌘+Shift+X** or by clicking **Filter > Liquify**. Click on the Zoom tool at the bottom of the Liquify toolbar, position over the lips, and click until the lips fill the preview screen. Select the Freeze Mask tool **(F)**, which is fourth from the bottom in Liquify's toolbar, and use it to paint a mask over the bottom lip. This will allow us to adjust the size of the top lip without affecting the lower one.

Freeze Mask Tool (F)

View Options
☑ Show Image   ☐ Show Mesh
Mesh Size: Medium
Mesh Color: Gray
☑ Show Mask
Mask Color: Green
☑ Show Backdrop
Use: All Layers
Mode: Behind
Opacity: 100

3 Tick the Show Backdrop box at the bottom of the View Options pane, so you can see the results of changes against the background. Choose the Bloat tool **(B)**, set the brush size to 85 pixels, position the cursor over one side of the top lip, and click to enlarge it. Repeat this process with the other side of the lip until you are happy. Remember, at this point we are only enlarging the top lip slightly to better match the other.

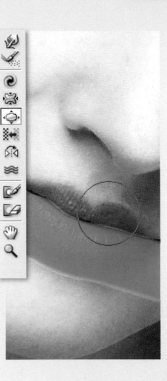

4 Thaw the mask covering the bottom lip with the Thaw Mask tool **(D)** and then reselect the Bloat tool. This time, set the brush size to 127 pixels and repeat the enlarging process in Step 3, this time over both lips. Once you are happy with the results, click on the OK button in the Liquify interface. Because the lips were on a separate layer, no changes were made to the background, giving you the opportunity to return to the original at any time. To finish, use a soft-edged eraser **(E)** to remove any unwanted areas of skin surrounding the lips in Layer 1 and then press **Ctrl/⌘+E** to flatten the image. The end result is subtle but seductive.

After

SUPERSTAR SMILE
Teeth whitening & straightening

Before

Dear Jane,

I've got a best friend called Becky. She is very outgoing, has a great personality and a wonderfully wicked sense of humor. With all this going for her you'd think she'd be fighting boys off with a stick, but in reality she hasn't had a date in ages. I think this is all because her teeth aren't very nice. She has a large gap between her two front teeth and they are also a little bit discolored. I've tried to persuade her to do something about them but she won't because she hates going to the dentist. I would be very grateful if you could show me a way to improve her teeth in Photoshop. I'm sure if she could see how pretty her teeth could look she would do something about them.

Yours sincerely,
Ashley

Nurse J. Peg says...

Dear Ashley,

If you want to give your friend Becky something to grin about, just follow my five-point plan for creating the perfect smile, and I guarantee she will visit the dentist before you can say "orthodontic realignment."

Best wishes,
Jane

P.S. Tell her to get that stick ready, because it looks like she's going to need it.

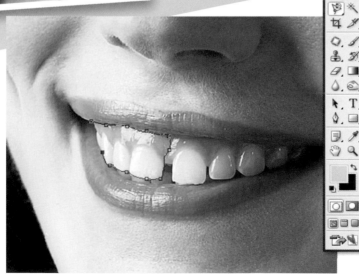

1 Select the Magnetic Lasso tool from the Toolbox. This is the third option in the Lasso tools sub-menu and can easily be identified by the magnet on the tool's icon. (Alternatively it can be selected by holding down the **Shift** key and repeatedly pressing **(L)** to scroll through the Lasso tool variations.) We will begin by using the Magnetic Lasso tool to make a selection of the teeth and gum on the left side of the picture. Click on the line where the gum meets the lip and drag the cursor along the line of the lip. As you draw with the mouse, you will see that a line appears following the edge of the lip, laying down anchor points to fasten the line to the edge. When you reach the center of the gum, drag the cursor down to follow the edge of the left front tooth, and carry on drawing around the teeth to complete the selection.

2 Right/control-click on the selection and choose Layer Via Copy from the pop up menu, or press **Ctrl/⌘+J**. This will make a copy of the selection and place it on a new layer, titled Layer 1. Return to the background layer and use the Magnetic Lasso to repeat the selection process on the right side group of teeth including the gum. Right/control-click on the selection and choose Layer Via Copy or press **Ctrl/⌘+J** to create a new layer, titled Layer 2.

3 Make sure that Layer 2 is positioned above Layer 1 and then press **Ctrl/⌘+T** to select the Free Transform command. Drag the center-left handle of the bounding box to the left in order to stretch the teeth selection and close the gap by half. Press **Return/↵** to apply the change, then repeat the stretching process with Layer 1, this time dragging the center-right handle of the bounding box to the right to fully close the gap.

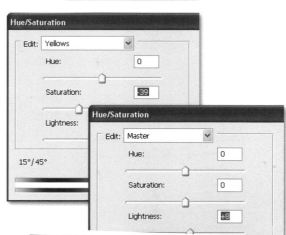

4 When happy with the repositioning of the teeth, make sure Layer 2 is active and go to **Layer > Merge Down** (or press **Ctrl/⌘+E**) to merge Layers 1 and 2 together. We can now turn our attention to whitening the teeth. Press **(L)** to select the Magnetic Lasso tool again and carefully draw a selection around the teeth, this time taking care not to select any of the gum.

5 Go to **Image > Adjustments > Hue/ Saturation** (or press **Ctrl/⌘+U**) to call up the Hue/Saturation dialog box. Choose Yellows from the drop-down menu and drag the Saturation slider to the left to remove any yellow tinge from the teeth. Return to the drop-down menu, choose Master, and drag the Lightness slider slightly to the right to lighten the teeth. Take care not to over-adjust the lightness control, as this will make the teeth look artificially white. When you are happy with the adjustments, click OK to apply the changes and **Ctrl/⌘+D** to deselect the teeth. Finally, flatten the image by selecting **Layer > Flatten Image**.

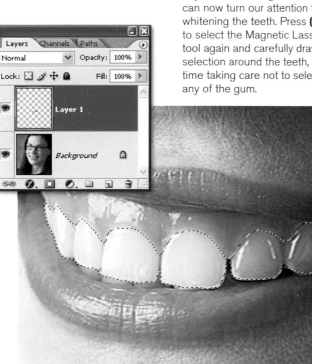

After

SKIN GLOW
A glamorous soft-focus look

Dear Jane,

I love to look through my women's magazines and daydream about being a famous model with perfect skin, wearing beautiful clothes, and being photographed in faraway exotic locations. I know it sounds silly but I think I've got what it takes to be a great model and just need the right breaks. I've decided to put together a portfolio of photographs to show model agencies.

My brother is taking the photographs and they are really good but there is one look I would like—a soft-focus, glowing kind of skin—which he says he can't achieve because he is saving up to buy a diffusing filter. I would be very grateful if you could show me a way to achieve this effect without the filter thingy.

Yours faithfully,

Justine

Nurse J. Peg says...

Dear Justine,

Tell your brother to follow my four straightforward stages to produce a glamorous soft-focus glow. Not only will it enhance your portfolio, but it will also save your brother from having to buy a filter thingy.

Regards,
Nurse J. Peg

Before

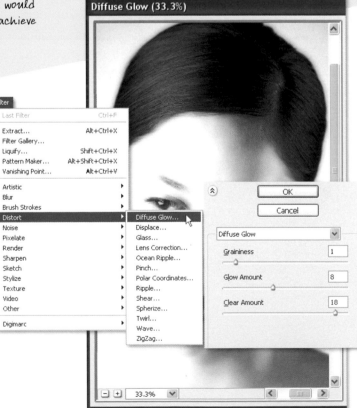
Diffuse Glow (33.3%)

1 Open the image in Photoshop and then immediately duplicate the background layer by dragging it onto the Create New Layer icon at the bottom of the Layers palette. Double-click on the layer and name it "Glow." Now go to **Filter > Distort > Diffuse Glow** to open the Diffuse Glow dialog box and enter the following settings: Graininess 1, Glow Amount 8, and Clear Amount 18. Click OK to apply the effect and return to the main Photoshop interface.

3 Return to the background layer and duplicate it once more by dragging it onto the Create New Layer icon at the bottom of the Layers palette. Name this layer "Blur" and place it above the Glow layer in the Layers palette. Now go to **Filter > Blur > Gaussian Blur**, enter a pixel radius amount of 15, and click OK to apply blur to the layer.

2 Although the Diffuse Glow filter has added an attractive glow to your portrait, it has also overblown the highlights in the process, losing most of the detail down the left side of the image. To remedy this, set the Glow layer's blending mode to Soft Light. This will return some of the detail to the image while retaining an underlying glow.

4 Reduce the opacity of the Blur layer to 50%. Now select the Eraser tool **(E)** from the Toolbox, go to the Tool Options bar, and set the brush opacity to 50%. Use a soft-edged brush to gently sharpen the eyes by erasing areas of the blur layer. This adds a central focus point to your completed image. Finally, combine the layers together by going to **Layer > Flatten Image**.

After

SKIN DEEP
Complexion perfection

Dear Jane,

I am a very enthusiastic amateur photographer, mainly interested in portraits. I've been experimenting lately with various lighting techniques and camera settings, with the aim of creating the perfect magazine-cover look. The effect I'm looking for is that of flawless natural beauty. I have used a number of different models but I always have the same problem: skin texture. No matter how good their complexion looks to the naked eye, or how much makeup they use, the camera always picks up fine lines, wrinkles, and blemishes.

Kind regards,
Mike

Nurse J. Peg says...

Dear Mike,

No matter how good your photography or how beautiful your models, you will never achieve a perfect magazine-cover portrait in camera. By following this example of how to produce a flawless complexion, you may well go some way to creating your perfect cover-style portrait. As for finding the perfect model who needs no retouching, I think you've got a better chance of finding a needle in a haystack.

Regards,
Nurse J. Peg

Before

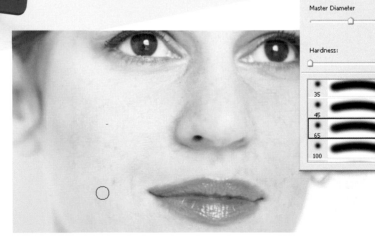

1 Open the image that you want to retouch, then select the Clone Stamp tool, either from the Toolbox or by pressing the **(S)** key. We will be using the Clone Stamp tool to remove any obvious spots and blemishes from the skin. Choose a soft-edged brush from the drop-down Brushes menu in the Tool Options bar and set the blending mode to Lighten, ensuring that only pixels darker than the sampled skin area will be replaced.

2 Place the cursor over an area of smooth skin near to the spot at the left side of the mouth, hold down the **Alt/⌥** key, and click to sample the skin area. Now move the cursor directly over the spot and click once to remove the blemish. Repeat this process to remove the remaining obvious blemishes, making sure to sample a smooth area of skin as near as possible to the blemish so that the skin tones will match.

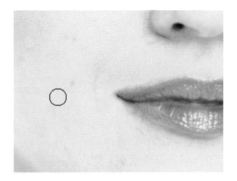

3 Once the blemish removal process has been completed, duplicate the layer by pressing **Ctrl/⌘+J** (or by going to **Layer > Duplicate Layer**). We will now add a blur effect to the new layer to soften the appearance of the skin. Open the Gaussian Blur filter dialog box by going to **Filter > Blur > Gaussian Blur**. Drag the

pixel radius slider to the right until the skin is visibly softened—in this example a radius of 10 pixels was sufficient. Click OK to apply the results of the filter to the new layer.

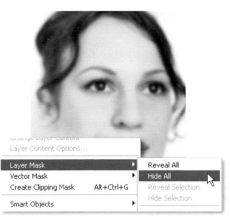

4 As you can see, this effect softens the skin but blurs facial details. We now need to apply the softened skin selectively. To do this, apply a layer mask to the copied layer by going to **Layer > Add Layer Mask > Hide All**. This will add a black mask to the image to hide the blurred layer, making the layer with facial details visible.

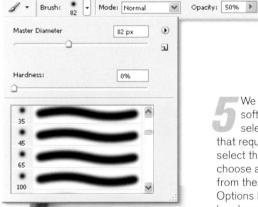

5 We can now apply the softened skin layer selectively to the areas that require it. To do this, select the Brush tool and choose a soft-edged option from the menu in the Tool Options bar. Reduce the brush opacity to 50% and select white as the paint color. Now paint away the mask over the areas of skin that need softening, making sure you retain the detail in the eyes, nose, and mouth. If too much of the mask is removed, switch the paint color to black and paint back the detail. Use the opacity of the brush to regulate the amount of softening applied.

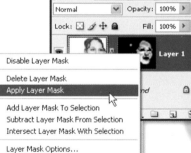

6 When you are happy with the results of the skin softening, right/control-click on the Layer mask in the Layers palette and choose Apply Layer Mask from the pop-up menu to apply the effects of the mask to the layer. Finally, merge the layers together by pressing **Ctrl/⌘+E** to complete the process of producing a perfect complexion.

After

THE COVER UP
Concealing spots & acne

Before

Hi Jane,

I need your help like yesterday! I'm 16 years old and have been hitting on this hot chick in an Internet chat room. We've been getting on like really well and she wants to meet me next week. She has e-mailed me a cool photo of herself so I will recognize her. Now she wants a photo of me and the only one I've got is like really sad.

In the picture my face is really spotty and greasy and I've got a giant zit. I just know if I send it to her she won't show up. I really need to improve the photo fast! You've got to help me Jane, my love life depends on it.

Thanks dude,

Jack

Nurse J. Peg says...

"

Hi Jack,

Looking at your picture I can see your dilemma. Don't despair though, just follow my guide to give your photo a complexion that will have any impressionable teenage girl dying to meet you. I've got one more piece of good advice for you: be sure to wear something warm on your first date— like a balaclava.

Regards, Jane

"

1 We will begin by first removing the most obvious zits and blemishes. Press the **(J)** key to select the Patch tool, check the Destination option is selected in the Tool Options Bar, and then click and drag the Patch tool to make a rectangular selection on the nose, above the small scar. Make sure you make the selection big enough to cover the scar when it is repositioned. Now drag the selection over the small scar and watch as the scar miraculously disappears. Repeat this process on all of the most noticeable spots and blemishes, making sure that the selection is made close to the blemish in each case.

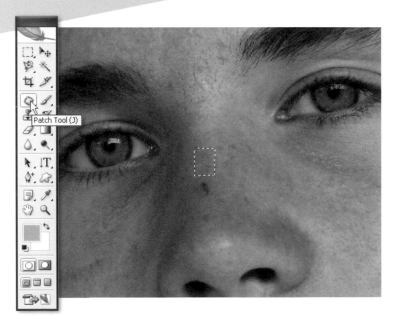

Patch Tool (J)

2 With all the main spots and blemishes removed, the skin is already looking better, but there is still a lot more we can do to improve it. Before that, we must duplicate the layer by going to the Layers palette and dragging the Background layer onto the New Layer Icon at the bottom of the palette. Now, working on the copy layer, press the **(B)** key to select the Brush tool, go to the Tool Options bar, set the blend mode to Darken, and lower the opacity of the brush to 50%. Hold down the **Alt/⌥** key to temporarily select the Eyedropper tool and click on a smooth area of skin to select a sample skin color. Release the **Alt/⌥** to return to the Brush tool and paint over the light areas of the skin. Painting in Darken mode replaces only the pixels that are lighter than the sample color; this makes it ideal for removing shine caused by oily skin or uneven lighting conditions.

3 Change the brush blend mode to Lighten and reduce the opacity to 30%. Painting in Lighten mode replaces only the pixels that are darker than the sample color. Make sure you keep resampling the skintone color as you paint over the different areas of the face. Painting separately with each blend mode has the overall effect of balancing out the skin tones to produce a flawless complexion.

After

4 As you can see, this process has cleaned up the skin but looks far too smooth and false. It may be suitable for a magazine cover, but not for a teenage boy wanting to impress. To remedy this simply reduce the opacity of the copy layer to about 75%. This will blend the layer with the original, allowing some of the original texture to show through, producing a more realistic appearance. Merge the layers together by pressing **Ctrl/⌘+E** to complete the transformation from spotty kid to handsome young man.

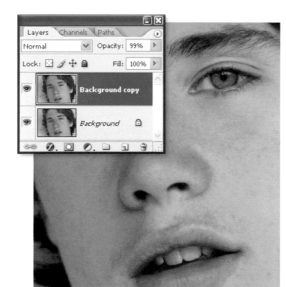

VANISHING POINT
Removing scars & blemishes

Dear Jane,

I am an active member of a local tennis club. I love to take part in competitions and was thrilled when my partner and I made it to the mixed doubles final of the annual charity tournament. We were winning two games to love in the first set when my partner swung his racket back and accidentally hit me on the top of my right cheek. Although it hurt, we carried on to win and I now have a wonderful photograph of me collecting the trophy with a nasty bruise on my face. I would love to frame and hang the photograph on my lounge wall but would like to try and remove the bruise first. Could you show me a simple way of doing this?

Yours faithfully,

Rachel

Nurse J. Peg says...

Dear Rachel,

Try this simple four-step technique. It's perfect for removing bruises and works just as well for the removal of birthmarks, skin pigmentation and embarrassing hickeys.

Regards,
Nurse J. Peg

Before

1 Open the image from which you would like to remove the bruise or birthmark, and then press the **(W)** key to select the Magic Wand tool. Go to the tool's options and set the tolerance level to 6, then click on the center of the bruise to roughly select it. You may need to add to the selection by holding down the **Shift** key and clicking again on an unselected area of the bruise.

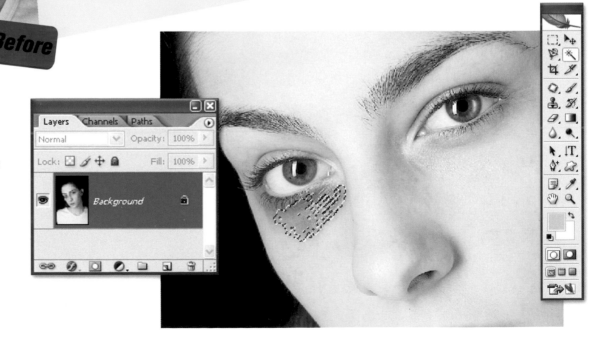

2 Press **Ctrl/⌘+Shift+I** or go to **Select > Inverse** to invert the selection and then press the **(Q)** key to enter Quick Mask mode. This will turn the selection into a blotchy red mask covering most of the bruise. Press the **(D)** key to make sure the default black and white foreground/background colors are selected and use the Brush tool to paint, with black, over any areas of the bruise that were not selected by the Magic Wand tool. Next go to **Filter > Blur > Gaussian Blur** and enter a radius of 12 pixels to blur the mask.

3 Press the **(Q)** key again to return to standard mode, followed by **Ctrl/⌘+Shift+I**, or go to **Select > Inverse** to once more invert the selection. Now go to **Image > Adjustments > Curves** or press **Ctrl/⌘+M** to open up the Curves dialog box.

4 You will notice that the cursor has now turned into an Eyedropper tool. Position the pointer over the darkest area of the bruise and then hold down the **Ctrl/⌘** key and click with the mouse to apply the corresponding pixel value to the curve. Press **Ctrl/⌘+H** to hide the selection border and then press the **Up/↑** arrow key a few times to lighten the selection and remove the bruise. Finally press **Ctrl/⌘+H** once more to return the selection border, and **Ctrl/⌘+D** to deselect.

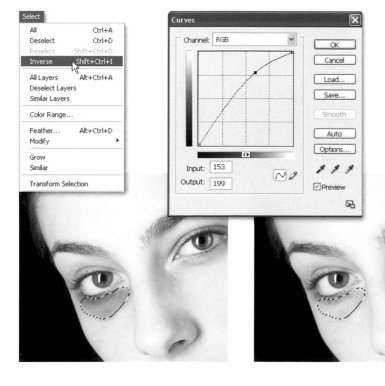

After

VIRTUAL TATTOO
Try before you buy

Dear Nurse Peg,

I've been thinking about getting a tattoo: nothing too big, just a simple heart with my boyfriend's name on it. The only problem is that I'm terrible at making decisions. First I can't decide what design to have, and second I can't decide where to have it. Can you recommend a simple Photoshop procedure that I can use to experiment with different designs and placement of virtual tattoos before going ahead with the real thing? I would hate to get a tattoo applied and then decide I don't like it.

Yours in anticipation,
Lola

Before

Nurse J. Peg says...

Dear Lola,

How sensible. So many people rush into a decision like this, then live to regret it or end up going through painful surgery to have the tattoo removed. Applying a virtual tattoo is a great way of seeing what a chosen design would look like before going through with it. You can create your own design and experiment with as many different boyfriends' names as you like. Just in case.

**Regards,
Nurse J. Peg**

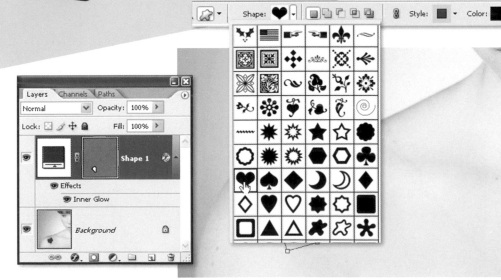

1 For this example we will create a simple tattoo using a combination of Photoshop's preset shapes. First, open the image on which to apply the tattoo, then hold down the **Shift** key while repeatedly pressing the **(U)** key until the Custom Shape tool is selected. Go to the Tool Options bar and choose the Heart Shape from the drop-down Custom Shape palette. Now click on the color box and choose a deep red from the Color picker dialog box. Click and drag the Shape tool to create a shape of a heart on the shoulder.

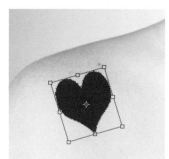

3 Return to the Custom Shape picker and choose Banner 1. Click and drag the Shape tool to create the shape. Press **Ctrl/⌘+T** to select the Free Transform tool and reposition the banner shape over the heart. Click on the color box and use the color picker to sample an area of skin near the tattoo. Double click the Shape 2 layer in the Layers palette to open the Layer Style dialog box, select Inner Glow, and change the opacity to 100% and the glow size to 15 pixels.

2 Using the Free Transform tool (**Ctrl/⌘+T**), reposition the heart shape on the shoulder. Double-click within the box to apply the change. Now double-click on the Shape 1 layer in the Layers palette to open the Layer Style dialog, box and select Inner Glow. Choose a deep blue for the glow color and set the opacity to 70%. Click on the radial button to select Edge as the glow source and set the size to 70 pixels. As you can see, this has applied a graduated blue edge to the heart shape.

4 Return once more to the Custom Shape picker and choose Arrow 3. Click and drag to create the shape and then use the Free Transform tool again to reposition the arrow so that it runs diagonally across the heart. Select **Layer > Rasterize > Shape** to change the arrow from a vector shape to a bitmap shape, allowing it to be edited with the Eraser tool.

Press the **(E)** key to select the Eraser, and use it to remove the center section of the shaft from the arrow to create the appearance of the arrow going through the heart.

5 Select the Starburst shape from the Custom Shape picker and apply it over the deleted end of the arrow shaft where it exits the heart (to create a stylized exit). Now add some text to complete the tattoo. Press the **(T)** key to select the Type tool and type your message; for this example we used the words "True Love" written in French script. Use the Free Transform tool and reposition the text so that it runs along the banner. Click on the Create Warped Text icon in the Tool Options bar, choose the Arc option from the drop-down Style menu, and apply a Horizontal bend of 10%.

6 Merge the tattoo design to a single layer by turning the background layer off (with the eye icon next to it), clicking Merge Visible from the Layers menu, then turning the background back on. Go to **Filter > Noise > Add Noise** and set the amount slider to 5%. Click OK. Next go to **Filter > Blur > Gaussian Blur** and set the radius slider to 0.5%. To complete the effect, choose the Darken blend mode from the Layers palette and set the layer opacity to 80%.

After

TATTOO TAKEAWAY
Seamless tattoo removal

Dear Jane,

About 10 years ago now I made the stupid mistake of getting tattoos on my back. At the time it seemed like a good idea but as I get older I'm growing to hate them. I've reached the point where I'm ashamed to take my shirt off in public, which is quite a problem as I work as a stripper. I have decided to have laser treatment to remove the tattoos. Although this will make me much happier, it will leave my portfolio of photographs out of date. If you could solve my problem, this would save me having to replace it.

Yours faithfully,
Ed

Nurse J. Peg says...

Dear Ed,

Removing tattoos from a photograph is a lot simpler than removing the real thing, as I'm sure you will appreciate after enduring hours of painful laser skin removal and chemical peels.

Regards,
Nurse J. Peg

Before

1 As you can see, this image contains two groups of tattoos that need removing. The set of Chinese characters on the left are relatively small and should not be any trouble to remove, so we shall tackle these first. Hold down **Shift** and press the **(L)** key twice to select the Polygon Lasso tool. Use the lasso to make a rectangular selection around the tattoo, select the Patch tool **(J)** from the Toolbox, and click on the Source radial button in the Tool Options bar. Next, drag the selection to the left. As you drag the selection, a preview of the potential patch appears above the tattoos—release the mouse when the new source looks good. Press **Ctrl/⌘+D** to deselect.

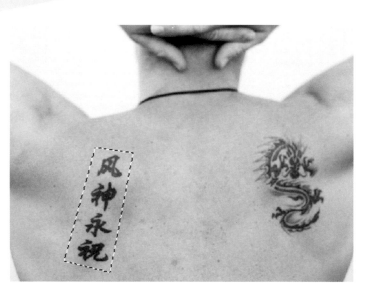

2 The results of the initial Patch are impressive and require only a few minor adjustments. Still using the Patch tool, click on the Destination radial button and make a selection of the shadow created by the shoulder blade. Drag the selection diagonally up to the left to fill in the lighter area that was left after the initial patch had been applied.

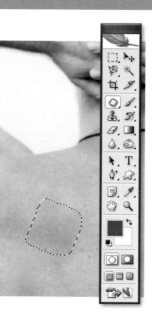

3 We can now turn our attention to the larger tattoo, which because of its size could be more problematic if we used the same technique. The remedy? Clone the clean area of skin from the left side of the back and position it over the right, covering the tattoo. To do this, select the Rectangular Marquee tool and make a selection of the left shoulder. Right/control-click on the selection and choose Layer Via Copy from the pop-up menu.

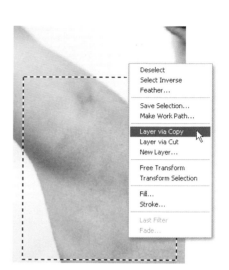

4 Go to **Edit > Transform > Flip Horizontal** and then reposition the copied selection of the left shoulder over the right shoulder. Reduce the opacity of Layer 1 to 80%. Then select the Free Transform tool by pressing **Ctrl/⌘+T** (or by going to **Edit > Free Transform**). Use the tool to rotate the selection in order to line it up perfectly with the right shoulder. Double-click inside the Free Transform bounding box to apply the changes, and return the Layer 1 opacity to 100%.

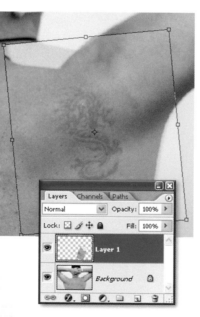

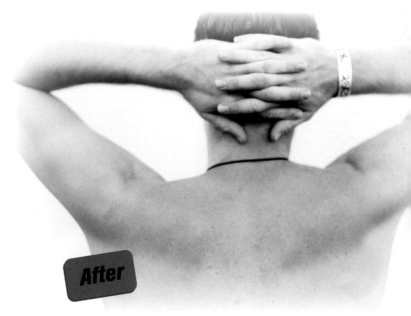

After

5 From the Layer menu select **Add Layer Mask > Reveal All** to apply a layer mask to Layer 1. Now use a black, soft-edged paintbrush to remove the unwanted areas of the mask. If too much of the mask is removed, paint with white to replace it. When you are happy with the outcome of the mask editing, apply the results by going to **Layer > Remove Layer Mask > Apply**. The layers can then be flattened to reveal a smooth back totally free from tattoos.

THE LIVING HIGHLIGHTS

Check out the blonde before the bleach

Before

Dear Jane,

I'm a dancer and have just been offered a position with a famous pop diva's dance troupe. We are due to set off on a world tour at the end of the month. The only problem is that they have asked me to have my hair highlighted before the start of the tour, as all the other girls in the troupe have lighter blonde hair. As I am a natural blonde already and have never colored my hair before, I am rather apprehensive about this. I would die if I hated the result. If I could see what my hair would look like after highlights have been added I would feel much happier about keeping my appointment with the hairstylist.

Yours nervously,
Carrie

Nurse J. Peg says...

Dear Carrie,

You are the only person I've met who can make an appointment at the hairdresser sound more like a visit to the dentist, but don't worry. Follow my easy-to-apply technique for creating beautifully highlighted hair, show the results to your stylist, and ask him to copy the results. If, after the real highlights have been applied, you are not happy with the results, you can always shave your hair off and wear a wig. After all, it'll grow back again. Eventually.

Regards,
Nurse J. Peg

1 To begin this very quick and simple technique for applying multi-tonal highlights to drab hair, press the **(Q)** key or click on the Quick Mask icon at the bottom of the Toolbox. Next, switch to the Brush tool **(B)**, right/control-click to open the brush options dialog, and choose a soft-edged brush 65 pixels wide.

Master Diameter | 65 px

Hardness: | 0%

35
45
65
100

2 Now paint a Quick Mask over separate sections, following the flow of the hair. Don't worry about being too precise, as we will sort this out later. Hit **(Q)** again to switch back to standard mode, and the area around the mask will become a selection. As we want the strands of hair to be selected instead, go to **Select > Inverse** to invert the selection.

3 Next, copy the selected sections of hair to a new layer by going to **Layer > New > Layer Via Copy** (or by pressing **Ctrl/⌘+J**). As the hair is now copied to a new layer, we can adjust its color without changing the underlying background layer. Go to **Image > Adjustments > Hue/Saturation** (or press **Ctrl/⌘+U**) to open the Hue/Saturation dialog box.

Drag the saturation slider to the right to increase the saturation of the selection by + 30 and then click OK to apply the change.

4 You can see that this instantly lifts the hair sections, but the overall effect looks a little clumsy. To soften the effect and make the hair look more natural, go to **Layer > Add Layer Mask > Reveal All**. Use a soft-edged, low-opacity brush **(B)** to paint with black over the edges of the hair strands to soften the effect and better blend the hair with the

background layer. Once you are satisfied with the results, try repeating the process with different strands of hair to build up a multi-tonal effect, or adjusting the hair layer color balance to add colored highlights.

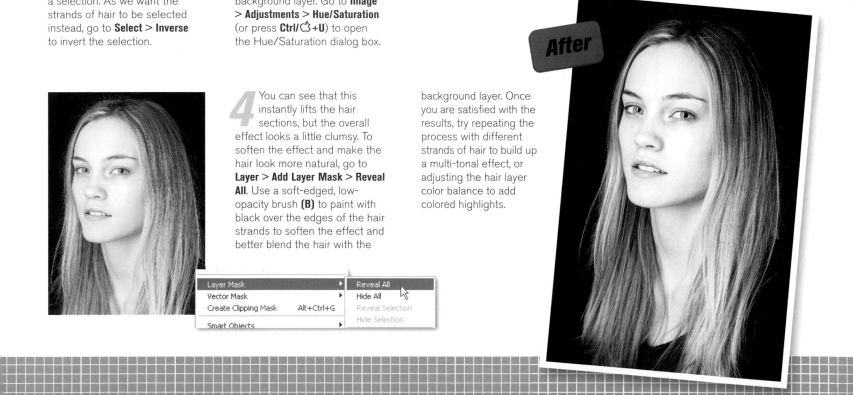

After

DYEING FOR A CHANGE
Taking the guesswork out of hair color

Hi Jane,

My name is Max and I'm a stylist in a hip salon. I specialize in hair coloring, and many of my clients leave it up to me to experiment with style and color. Most of the time this works out fine, but on occasions some of them have been a little shocked by the results. I recall one particular client saying, "I wish I could have seen what it was going to look like before you started." This gave me the idea of offering a preview service. I already have a large number of hairstyles on the computer, which I simply layer on top of the client's image. What I'm not sure how to achieve is the application of color to the various styles. I would be very grateful if you could help me (and my clients).

Yours in anticipation,
Max

Nurse J. Peg says...

Dear Max,

What a good idea! I can't tell you how often I've wished I'd had the chance to see my new style before they started snipping. Photoshop has the perfect solution: the Color Replacement tool, which allows you to change any color in an image without losing its tonal qualities. Take a look at my example, then try it on your clients. Just don't be offended if they then decide to go to a different salon.

Regards,
Nurse J. Peg

Before

1 We will start by making a simple selection of the hair with the Magic Wand tool. Select the Magic Wand tool from the Toolbox or by pressing the **(W)** key and clicking on the white background to select it. Then hold down the **Shift** key while clicking with the mouse on the background between the spikes of hair to add to the selection. Press **Ctrl/⌘+Shift+I** (or go to **Select > Inverse**) to switch the selection from the background to the hair. Now press **Ctrl/⌘+J** to copy the selection to a new layer.

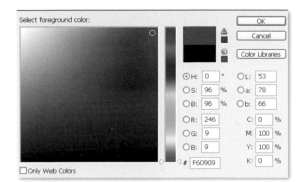

2 Now to change the hair color. For this example we will be using the Color Replacement tool, which can be found in the Toolbox, grouped with the Healing Brush and Patch tools, or can be selected via the **(J)** key. Once we have the Color Replacement tool selected, we need to choose a suitable replacement color. Click on the foreground color in the Toolbox—this will open the color picker dialog box. Here I picked a bright red as the replacement color.

3 Now go to the Tool Options bar: set the Mode option to Color and the sampling option to Once. This will confine the color replacement to the color of the pixels that are first clicked on. As you paint over the hair with the Color Replacement tool, you will see that all the original shadows and highlights are preserved as the color of the pixels change. Continue painting until all the hair color has been replaced. If you want to experiment with other colors on the same head, simply open the Color Picker by clicking on

the Foreground color box and select another color. When you are happy with the results, press **Ctrl/⌘+E** to flatten the image.

4 While the Color Replacement tool is great for making bold color changes such as this, it can also be used much more subtly, as with this blonde woman. The same technique has been used to add multi-tonal highlights to the hair and brighten up its appearance.

Example 2

After

RISE AND SHINE
Adding body and shine to your hair

Dear Jane,

I have a major problem: shampoo. I can't choose between shampoos containing ultra-rich amino acid complexes, moisturizing herbal antioxidants, PH-balanced formulas, hydrating botanical extracts, or nourishing vitamin infusions. I have tried dozens of these expensive shampoos, each promising to rejuvenate, revitalize, and reinvigorate my hair by adding extra body, vitality, and shine, but the only difference I can find between them is their smell.

In your professional opinion, do any of these ingredients actually work, or are they just made up by the big pharmaceutical companies to sell more soap?

Yours sincerely,
Janet

Nurse J. Peg says...

Dear Janet,

How would I know? I'm a nurse, not a chemist. What I do know, though, is the perfect formula for creating beautiful, voluminous hair with extra shine in a matter of minutes. My advice to you is put out of your mind all thoughts of key aminos, nutri-seramides and anti-liposomes and thoroughly apply my four-stage Photoshop formula to all your photographs. Follow this advice and I guarantee you will never have a bad hair day again.

Regards,
Nurse J. Peg

Before

1 Open your image in Photoshop and then go to **Filter > Liquify** or press **Ctrl/⌘+Shift+X** to open up the Liquify command interface. Select the Freeze Mask tool **(F)**, which can be found fourth from the bottom on the left-side tool bar, and use this to paint a green mask over the woman's face. By applying a freeze mask we are protecting the face from any distortions that will be made to the hair.

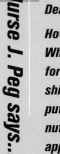

2 Now select the Bloat tool **(B)**, fifth from the top, and choose a brush size that is big enough to cover the width of the hair on the left side of the head. Position the brush cursor over the hair and click. You will see the area of hair covered by the brush expand slightly, and each time you click the mouse the hair will expand farther. Holding down the mouse button will expand the hair quickly, but for subtle changes such as the effect we are creating I prefer to use the slower click method.

3 Don't worry if you apply too much expansion to any part of the image, as the Reconstruct options give you a variety of ways to reverse the distortions made to the image. If you are not happy with any of the distortions applied, simply click on the Restore All button to start again. When you are happy with the amount of volume added to the hair, click OK to exit the Liquify interface and apply the distortions to the image.

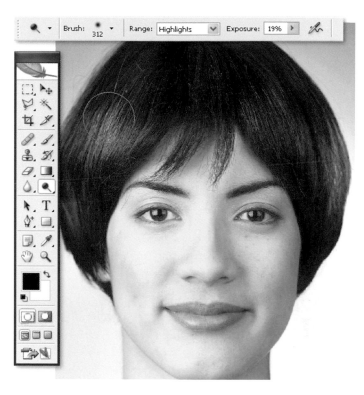

4 Now we have added extra body to the hair, let's boost the shine. Press the **(O)** key to select the Dodge tool from the Toolbox and choose a brush size slightly smaller than the width of the newly expanded hair. Set the brush exposure to around 20% and the range to Highlights. Brush over the hair to lighten the highlights and then set the exposure to 10% and the range to Midtones. Brush over the hair again to slightly lighten its midtones. Finally, hold down the **Shift** key as you press the **(O)** key again to select the Burn tool. Set the exposure to 10% and, the range to Shadows, and brush over the hair to darken the shadows. The resulting appearance is that of thick, shiny, and healthy hair.

After

A CHANGE OF STYLE
Try out your dream hair

Dear Jane,

I have a demanding job in a busy attorney's office. Punctuality is essential, as is good grooming, and readying myself for work can place quite a strain on my schedule. My hair is the largest drain on my time—it takes an inordinate amount of time to wash and blow-dry. I have considered having it restyled many times but have always reneged on my intentions. I would be extremely grateful if you could advise me on a procedure whereby I had the ability to pre-visualize any changes I could feasibly consider making to my hair.

Yours faithfully,
Melissa

Before

Nurse J. Peg says...

Dear Melissa,

If I understand you correctly, you would like to restyle your hair without actually cutting it? Well, to answer you in language that you'll understand: This proposal generates absolutely no predicament for Photoshop's versatile Clone Stamp tool and by replicating the rudimentary techniques expressed in the subsequent steps you will discover it possible to construct numerous adaptations to your current design. Getting you to speak plain English may be more difficult.

Regards,
Nurse J. Peg

1 The first step is to define the shape of the new style by making it into a selection. Press the **(P)** key to select the Pen tool and begin drawing a path. Click to add anchor points as you go around the top of the head. We only need a rough outline at the top, but as you come farther down the head, draw the path into the hair, following the flow to define the shape of the new style.

2 Complete the path by joining it up with the start point, and then right-click within the path and choose Make Selection from the pop-up menu. Now go to **Select > Inverse** or press **Ctrl/⌘+Shift+I** to invert the selection. We can now begin the process of cloning. At first glance this may seem a daunting prospect, especially given the amount of hair detail on the shirt, but by approaching the task slowly and methodically we can produce remarkable results.

3 Select the Clone Stamp tool by pressing the **(S)** key. Choose a soft-edged brush from the Tool Options bar, hold down the **Alt/⌥** key, and click on the gray background near to the hair to select a sample point. Clone the gray background over the hair—don't worry about going over the selection area with the clone tool, as only the area within the selection will be altered.

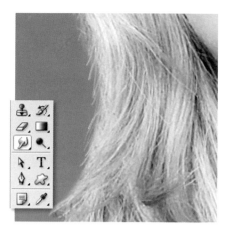

4 We can now turn our attention to the shirt. Press **Ctrl/⌘** and **+** to zoom into the right side of the shirt, then hold down the **Alt/⌥** key while clicking on a plain hairless section to select a sample point. Reduce the size of the brush and clone upward on one section of the shirt at a time, sampling as close to the clone area as possible so that the correct tone of the shirt is always retained. As you reach the edge of the shirt, harden the brush to produce a sharper line between the shirt and the background.

5 We can see the success of cloning the right side of the shirt; now repeat the process with the left side, again making sure to sample as close to the clone area as possible. When tackling the open neck area of the shirt, use a large brush, select a sample point that straddles the shirt and the skin area, and then clone upward, keeping the neckline straight. When all the shirt has been cloned, press **Ctrl/⌘+D** to deselect and use the Clone tool with a soft-edged brush to soften any jagged areas of the hairline.

6 Select the Smudge tool by pressing the **(R)** key, set the brush size to 1 pixel, and go around the hairline dragging out single strands of hair to create a more convincing, natural look. Finally use the Burn tool **(O)** to selectively darken areas of the shirt.

After

DIGITAL NAIL POLISH
Perfect polish after the party

Dear Nurse Peg,

Can you help me with a sticky problem? I recently organized and hosted a corporate charity ball. It was vital that the occasion went smoothly as we had a large number of VIPs on the guest list, and any problems would reflect badly on me. You can imagine my horror when I viewed the photographs that were taken on the night and realized that my nail polish clashed with my dress. I had been so busy organizing everything I had forgotten to change the color of my nails to match the expensive designer dress that I had bought for the occasion. Now I have to choose a number of photographs to appear in the monthly industry magazine, and if I can't change the color of my nails I will be the laughing stock of the corporation and my whole industry.

Yours desperately,
Alexis

Before

Nurse J. Peg says...

Dear Alexis,

Don't worry, just follow my four routine steps to perfect matching nail color and I guarantee that you will be the belle of the ball—providing the bitchy, back-stabbing e-mail campaign hasn't already been started by jealous business colleagues who were actually there to witness your fatal fashion faux pas.

**Best of luck,
Nurse J. Peg**

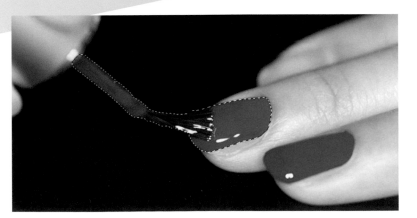

1 After opening the image in Photoshop, hold down the **Alt/⌥** key and then press the **(L)** key twice to select the Magnetic Lasso tool from the Toolbox. Click on the edge of the nail varnish brush and trace the outline of the brush and applied nail varnish. As you do this, the selection border will automatically snap to the edge of the fingernail. When the fingernail and brush have been selected, hold down the **Shift** key to allow you to add the other two fingernails to the selection.

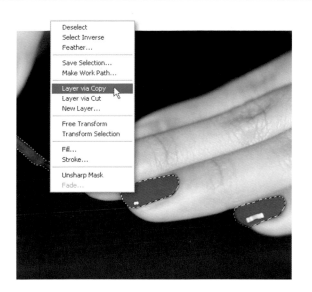

2 If the selection border runs off the line, retrace your steps while pressing the **Delete** key to delete the anchor points one at a time until you are back on line. Anchor points can also be added manually, as often as you need, by clicking the mouse. Once all the fingernails have been selected, right/control-click within the selection and choose Layer Via Copy from the pop-up menu (or press **Ctrl/⌘+J**) to copy the selection to a new layer. Rename the layer "Fingernails" by double-clicking on the name in the Layers palette.

3 Now we can use an adjust-ment layer with a clipping mask to change the color. Click on the New Fill or Adjustment Layer icon at the bottom of the Layers palette, and choose Selective Color. When the Selective Color dialog box appears, click OK to close it. Apply the clipping mask to the adjustment layer by holding down the **Alt/⌥** key and hovering between the fingernail and adjustment layers. When the pointer turns into two overlapping circles, click to clip the adjustment layer to the fingernails. Now any color adjustments made will apply only to the fingernails.

4 Double-click on the adjustment layer's thumbnail to bring up the Selective Color dialog box and select Reds from the drop-down colors menu. Now have fun adjusting the four color sliders to create an infinite number of shades for your digital nail polish. Once you have achieved the desired color, go to **Layer > Flatten Image** to compress the layers and apply the color adjustments.

After

HANDSOME HANDS
Remove veins, hair and wrinkles

Before

Dear Jane,

I have been the lady captain of an exclusive golf club for a number of years now and I very much enjoy the position of authority I hold. One of my happy duties is to present the winner of the annual ladies' tournament with a beautiful silver trophy which is engraved with her name and kept in the trophy cabinet along with a photograph of the presentation.

When first viewing the latest winner's photograph I was horrified to see unsightly veins protruding from the back of my hand as the glorious moment of passing over the trophy was captured. I really cannot allow this photograph to be displayed in the club without the removal of the offending veins.

Yours faithfully,
Patricia Hardwick-Smyth (Lady Captain)

Nurse J. Peg says...

Dear Pat,

Invisibly removing protruding veins from the back of hands is not a problem for Photoshop. Order one of your minions to follow these simple steps, and your glorious image will once more be gracing the trophy cabinet where it belongs.

Regards,
Nurse J. Peg

1 Open the image of the hand that you wish to retouch, and then go to the Toolbox and choose the Healing Brush tool **(J)**. In the Tool Options bar, set the mode to Lighten and choose a soft-edged brush, slightly wider than the vein you wish to remove. Hold down the **Alt/⌥** key and click to sample a smooth area of skin next to the first target vein, then stroke along its unsightly length with the brush, removing its darker, shadowy areas. Don't worry about the lighter areas of the veins at this point, as we will return to these later.

2 The Healing Brush automatically measures the texture, color, and luminosity of the source point, and then matches this information to that of the destination area, producing a seamless blend. In Lighten mode the Healing Brush will only blend the sample area with the darker parts of the destination area. Most of the time this will work fine, but occasionally the blend can be less than perfect. To rectify this, click **Edit > Fade Healing Brush** (or press **Ctrl/⌘+Shift+F**). When the Fade dialog box appears, drag the slider to the left to reduce the effects of the Healing Brush.

3 Once all the darker areas have been successfully removed, return to the Tool Options bar and change the mode setting to Darken. Now repeat the process of setting a sample point and painting over each vein. This time only the remaining lighter areas of each vein will be blended with the sample area, completing the vein removal process.

4 Now that the veins have been removed, you may find it necessary to use the Patch tool **(J)** to tidy the top section of each finger where the Healing Brush has not been as successful and left the fingers looking a little bit lumpy. Use the Patch tool to draw a selection around a blemish-free area of each finger, and then drag it onto the lumpy section to blend with the sample point, remove the lumps, and finalize the image.

After

MAGIC MANICURE
Fix your fingernails fast!

Before

Dear Jane,
My boyfriend recently asked me to marry him. It was so romantic when he got down on one knee in the middle of a packed restaurant. When I said "yes," all the customers cheered and the restaurant manager brought us over a bottle of champagne on the house to celebrate. He has bought me the most beautiful engagement ring which, even though it is a little tight, must have cost him a packet, and he wants to send a photograph of me wearing it to his parents in Australia. The problem is, I must have the worst fingernails in the world. I'm always biting them and would be really embarrassed for them to see how awful they are, especially next to their son's beautiful ring. Could you give me any tips to help me improve my fingernails on the photograph before my fiancé sends it to his parents?
Yours faithfully,
Monika

Nurse J. Peg says...

Dear Monika,

The best way to improve chipped and cracked fingernails in the real world is to stick on false ones, and that is exactly what we will do here. My tip for you is to apply the following four-stage Photoshop technique to create fantastic artificial nails on your image. Your future mother-in-law will be just as impressed with your shiny new nails as she is with her son's beautiful ring.

Regards,
Nurse J. Peg

1 The ideal tool for creating false nails is the Pen tool; select it from the Toolbox by pressing the **(P)** key and position the cursor at the base of the left edge of the fingernail. Click and then reposition the cursor to create a straight path running along the side of the fingernail, extending out past the end of the nail. Click to add an anchor point and reposition the pointer at a right angle to the path. When the path is lined up with the opposite edge of the nail, click to add an anchor point and reposition to form a rectangle with the starting point. Click to add an anchor point, then click on the starting point to complete the path, but this time hold down the mouse button and drag away at an angle from the anchor point. As you drag, two handles appear from the anchor point, and the last section of the path begins to curve. Drag the handles until the curve matches that of the fingernail.

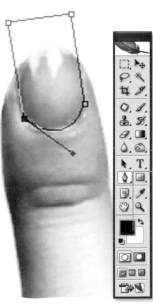

Plastic Wrap

Highlight Strength   1

Detail   15

Smoothness   13

2 Now we have a basic shape for the false nail we can adjust the shape to create any shape or style of fingernail. In this example I'm creating a French manicured fingernail, which has a squared-off end and a distinctive white tip. Go to the Toolbar and choose the Convert Anchor Point tool (often hidden behind the Pen tool), click on the anchor point at the top left of the path, and drag the handle up to curve the top edge of the path. Repeat this process with the top right anchor point until the top edge of the path is evenly curved between the two points.

3 Right/control-click within the path and select Make Selection from the pop-up menu. Then, click on the New Layer icon at the bottom of the Layers palette to place the selection on a new layer. Now click on the Foreground color at the bottom of the Tools palette to open the Color Picker dialog box and select a soft pink. Fill the selection by pressing **Shift+F5** or by going to **Edit > Fill** and then choosing Fill With Foreground Color from the pop-up dialog box.

4 Press the **(B)** key to select the Brush tool, switch the foreground and background colors to make white the new foreground color, and then paint over the tip of the nail to create the French manicured look. Press **Ctrl/⌘+D** to deselect, then press the **(O)** key to select the Dodge tool. Use this to gently

brush over the center of the nail to create highlights. To give the fingernails a slightly more glossy look, go to **Filter > Artistic > Plastic Wrap** and adjust the sliders until a realistic, glossy look is achieved.

When you are happy with the results of a single fingernail, repeat the process for each finger, or do as I did with these two finished examples and simply copy the completed fingernail to a new layer for each finger, and use the Free Transform tool to resize and position it over the original fingernails.

After

Example 2

CONTENTS

SECTION 3

Eternal Youth

Cheat the march of time with Dr. Jackson's timeless techniques for turning back the clock

THE CLASSIC FACELIFT
Smooth away the years

Dear Dr. Jackson,

Twenty-five years of cooking, cleaning, and taking care of my husband, four children, two dogs, and a rabbit have taken their toll on my body and mind. I feel like an extra from Invasion of the Body Snatchers. I need some Me time, I need to be pampered, I need romance, but most of all I need a facelift.

Yours hopefully, Brenda

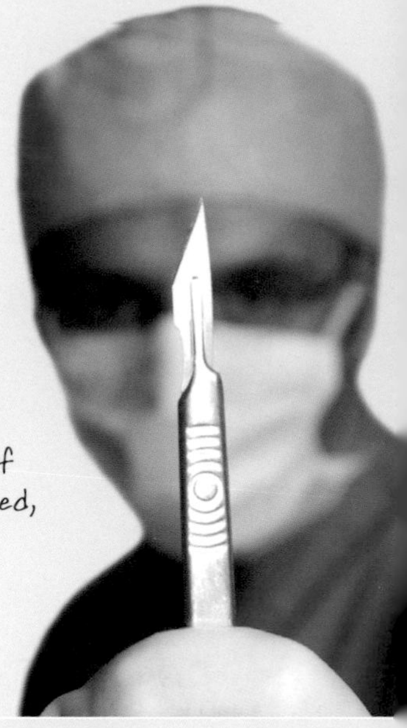

Dr. Jackson says...

"**Dear Brenda,**

I recommend you apply a liberal dose of my four-step facelift technique to a recent photograph of yourself. This will allow you to see just how wonderful you would look now if you hadn't married and had children and pets. It can't show you whether you would be a bitter, childless spinster instead, however.

**Kind regards,
Dr. B. Jackson**"

Before

Master Diameter | 188 px

Hardness: | 69%

1 Open the image you wish to apply the facelift procedure to, and press the **(Q)** key to enter Quick Mask mode, followed by the **(D)** key to ensure the default black and white, foreground/background colors are selected. Now select the Brush tool **(B)** from the Toolbox, go to the Tool Options bar, select a large brush, and set the hardness of the brush's edge to around 70%. Paint with black to apply a red mask over the lower half of the woman's face, before pressing the **(X)** key to switch the foreground color to white, then painting to erase the mask and define the shape of the woman's jawline.

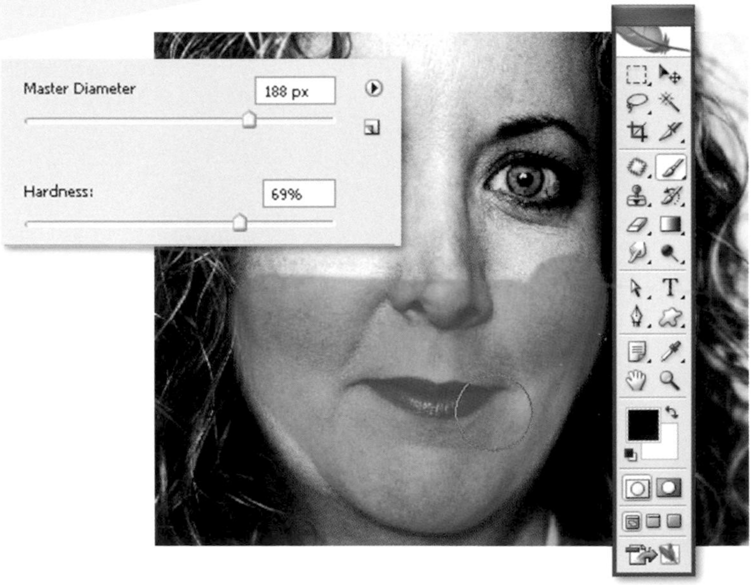

2 Hit the **(Q)** key again to return to standard mode and you will see the mask turn into a selection. Go to **Select > Inverse (Ctrl/⌘+Shift+I)** to switch the selection area from around the jaw to the jaw itself, before pressing **Ctrl/⌘+J** to copy it to a new layer.

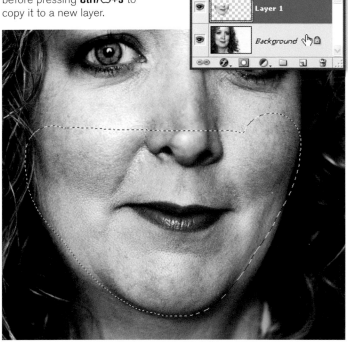

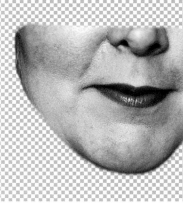

3 Turn off the background layer by clicking on the eye icon to the left of it in the Layers palette; this will let you preview the shape of the new fat-free jawline. If you are satisfied with the results, turn the background layer back on and carry on to the next stage. If you are not satisfied with the results, you can edit the shape by using the Eraser **(E)** to remove areas of the image, and the History Brush tool **(Y)** to return them, before turning the background layer back on.

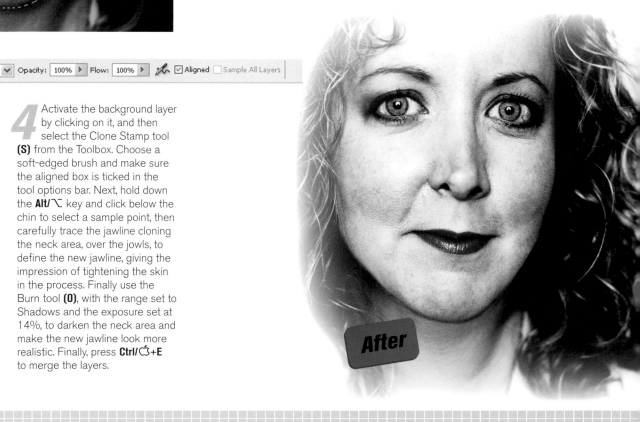

4 Activate the background layer by clicking on it, and then select the Clone Stamp tool **(S)** from the Toolbox. Choose a soft-edged brush and make sure the aligned box is ticked in the tool options bar. Next, hold down the **Alt/⌥** key and click below the chin to select a sample point, then carefully trace the jawline cloning the neck area, over the jowls, to define the new jawline, giving the impression of tightening the skin in the process. Finally use the Burn tool **(O)**, with the range set to Shadows and the exposure set at 14%, to darken the neck area and make the new jawline look more realistic. Finally, press **Ctrl/⌘+E** to merge the layers.

After

SAGGING SOLUTION
Giving you the lift you need

Dear Dr. Jackson,

Since my late teens I've led a wild life consisting of late nights, fast cars, fast food, and even faster women. All this has been washed down with copious amounts of alcohol. Throughout this high life I've rarely worried about my health or appearance, until I recently caught sight of my ravaged reflection. This has made me realize that I should finally regain control of my life and get back in shape. I have come up with a strict diet and exercise plan but I'm having difficulty motivating myself to start my new regime. I would be very grateful if you could possibly show me how I would look after sticking to my plan.

Kind regards,

Frank

Before

Dr. Jackson says...

Dear Frank,

Judging by your photograph I think you are embarking on this plan of action not a minute too soon, and maybe a good few years too late. But what the hell, at least it sounds like you've had a good time. As for giving you the incentive to start your new fitness regime, simply follow my six-step strategy to see how you would look if you had taken your mother's advice sooner.

Kind regards,
Dr. B. Jackson

1 The most versatile tool for lifting sagging skin or reducing chubby cheeks is Photoshop's Liquify tool; it enables us to perform many complex changes and distortions to an image, which are then only applied to the original when you are satisfied with the results. To begin our sagging skin reduction, open the image in Photoshop and then press **Ctrl/⌘+Shift+X** or go to **Filter > Liquify** to open the Liquify command interface.

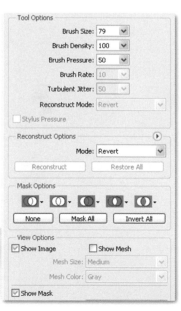

Tool Options

Brush Size: 79
Brush Density: 100
Brush Pressure: 50
Brush Rate: 10
Turbulent Jitter: 50
Reconstruct Mode: Revert

☐ Stylus Pressure

Reconstruct Options

Mode: Revert

Reconstruct   Restore All

Mask Options

None   Mask All   Invert All

View Options

☑ Show Image   ☐ Show Mesh

Mesh Size: Medium
Mesh Color: Gray

☑ Show Mask

2 We will start by reducing the sagging skin below the chin. Select the Forward Warp tool **(W)** from the top of the toolbar, and starting with a brush size of approximately 190 pixels, gently push the sagging skin upward toward the jawline. Increase the brush size and repeat this until you have a smooth, flab-free jawline.

3 Now change to the Push Pixels Left tool **(O)**. Select a smaller brush size and then position the cursor adjacent to the right cheek. Drag the mouse upward in one smooth stoke to push the background pixels left, instantly slimming the chubby right cheek. If you don't get this right, click the reconstruct button and try again.

4 Next, press the **(F)** key to select the Freeze Mask tool and paint over the man's moustache—this will protect the moustache from any distortions made to the surrounding area. Now press the **(S)** key to select the Pucker tool, increase the brush size to 522 pixels, and position the tool over the man's left cheek. Click the mouse button a couple of times and you will notice the area covered by the brush is sucked inward, reducing the size of the cheek.

5 The man's face is now looking much slimmer, but the half-closed right eye still gives the impression of chubbiness; to rectify this, we will open the eye more. Press the **(W)** key to select the Forward Warp tool once again, and set the brush size to 49 pixels. Position the cursor over the right eye and drag the edge of the lower eyelid downward to open the eye wider. You will notice this smudges the pupil, but don't worry, we will remedy this later. Click OK to apply all the distortions.

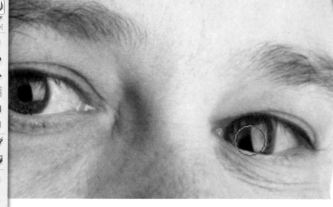

6 Zoom into the eye area and press the **(M)** key to select the Elliptical Marquee tool, drag across the left pupil to select it, and then press **Ctrl/⌘+J** to copy it to a new layer. Select the move tool **(V)** and drag the new pupil, positioning it over the left one. Next, use a soft-edged eraser **(E)** to carefully erase the edges of the pupil to blend with the background. Finally, merge the layers.

After

JAW DROPPING
Stronger jawline in minutes

Dear Dr. Jackson,

I've heard on the grapevine that you are the man to talk to regarding cosmetic surgery procedures. If so, I was wondering if you could help me with my problem?

I have got a weak chin. I realize most people wouldn't see this as any big deal and I have to say it doesn't actually affect me physically in any way, such as giving me a speech impediment or making it difficult for me to eat. What it has done is affect my mental well-being. I hate the look of my jawline, especially the side view, and I can't bear to look at myself in photographs or reflective surfaces because my appearance upsets me too much.

I would love to have a firm, strong jawline. Not only would it greatly improve my appearance, but it would also do wonders for my self-esteem. I do hope I have found the right man for the job and that you can give me the results I desire.

Yours hopefully,

Peter

Before

Dr. Jackson says...

Dear Peter,

Keep your chin up, you've come to the right man! For this particular problem I can recommend not just one but two extremely quick and easy procedures. I suggest you apply the following simple steps to all your photographs and paste them over every mirror and reflective surface in your home. It will then only be a matter of time before you begin to believe what you see and your mental well-being will greatly improve.

Regards,
Dr. B. Jackson

1 To strengthen the jawline, we will begin by selecting the Freehand Lasso tool **(L)** from the Toolbox. Use this to draw a rough selection around the jaw, and then right/control-click within the selection and choose Layer Via Copy from the pop-up menu to place the selection on a new layer. Now press **Ctrl/⌘+T** to apply the Free Transform bounding box to the selection.

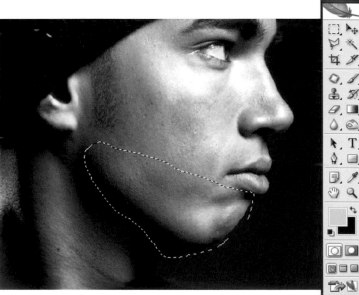

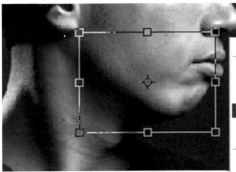

2 Right/control-click within the bounding box and choose the Distort option from the pop-up menu. Drag the bottom right handle of the bounding box diagonally down to the right to lengthen the jaw, then push the top right handle diagonally down to the left to ensure the outline of the chin lines up with the lower lip. Press the **Return/↵** key to apply the transformation, and use a low-opacity soft-edged Eraser **(E)** to blend the edges of the layer with the background. Finally, press **Ctrl/⌘+E** to merge the layers together to complete this version of the transformation from weak chinned to firm jawed.

3 My second example of strengthening the jawline is even quicker and simpler than the first, but still produces the same flawless results. Start by going to **Filter > Liquify** or press **Ctrl/⌘+Shift+X** to open up the Liquify command interface. From the top of the toolbar choose the Forward Warp tool **(W)** and set the brush size to around 360 pixels. Position the cursor over the chin and drag the mouse diagonally down and to the right to elongate the chin. When happy with the new shape of the jawline, click OK to apply the distortions and complete our alternative transformation in double-quick time.

After

Example 2

DOUBLE TROUBLE
Eradicate that double chin

Dear Dr. Jackson,

Please can you help me? I'm in my mid-forties and middle-aged spread has set upon me with a vengeance. Not only have I piled on the pounds around my midriff, but my face has also filled out, leaving me with fleshy jowls and a double chin that is most evident when I laugh. Because of my hectic work and social life I find it very difficult to fit in any kind of lasting exercise regime and my only contact with sports these days is watching football on TV, accompanied by a six-pack of beer. Can you recommend to me a proven fat-reduction system that would return my face to its pre-flab glory?

Kind regards,

David

Before

Dr. Jackson says...

Dear David,

I recommend that you follow my fat-busting five-step plan to creating firmer jowls and think about taking up an active hobby that you could incorporate into your busy work and social life, such as cycling to work or jogging to the bar. That way you could lose a few pounds—but you may also lose a few friends and work colleagues, who won't appreciate your new cologne, "Eau de sweat." So, on second thoughts, it may be wiser just to go with the flow and try not to laugh.

All the best,
Dr. B. Jackson

1 To begin the process of removing David's fleshy jowls, press **Ctrl/⌘+Space** to zoom into the double chin area and then hit the **(P)** key to select the Pen tool from the Toolbox. We can now use the Pen tool to draw a path through the fleshy area of the chin to determine a new jawline. Click just below the chin to start the path and then drag the mouse to create the shape of the new jawline, clicking and dragging to add anchor points and curve the path.

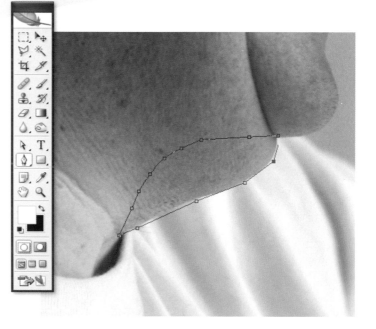

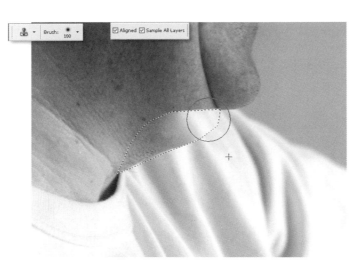

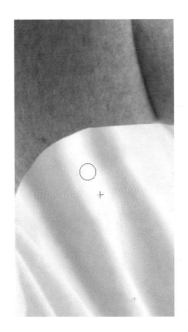

Create vector mask
Delete Path

Define Custom Shape...

Make Selection...

Fill Path...
Stroke Path...

Clipping Path...

Free Transform Path

2 Close the path by returning to the start point along the bottom of the fleshy chin line, and then right/control-click within the closed path and choose Make Selection from the pop-up menu. This will now enable you to edit the area within the selection without affecting the area outside the selection.

3 Press the **(S)** key to select the Clone Stamp tool and choose a large, soft-edged brush. Hold down the **Alt/⌥** key and mouse click on the T-shirt below the selection to create a sample point, then position the cursor over the selection and click and drag the mouse across the selection to clone the sampled T-shirt over the fleshy double chin.

4 Press **Ctrl/⌘+D** to deselect, then reduce the brush size of the Clone tool to around 25 pixels and the opacity to about 40%. Clone over any obvious joins between the original T-shirt and the newly cloned area until the whole T-shirt area becomes one and looks natural.

5 Although the jawline has been reshaped, we can see that the deep crease running down the face still gives the impression of a double chin. To remedy this, select the Patch tool **(J)** from the Toolbox and draw a selection around the crease. Make sure that the Source button is checked and then drag the patch selection to the right, over a crease-free area of the cheek. As you drag, you will see that the area the patch is dragged to replaces that of the original selection, removing the crease and blending it into the surrounding cheek area.

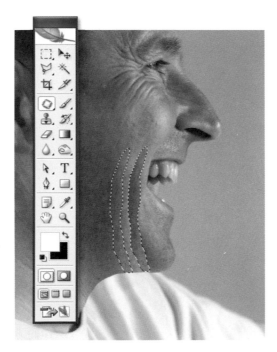

After

THE EYELIFT
Banishing baggy eyes

Dear Dr. Jackson,

Having spent most of my life as a missionary in Africa I have not had the time, inclination, or indeed the resources to waste on following even the simplest of beauty regimes. As a result my eyes have become lined and baggy, making me look much older than my years. I am just about to publish a book chronicling my life as a missionary and I'm also about to embark on a small tour of the UK, giving lectures about my time in Africa to charitable organizations. I would like to use a specific photograph of myself on a poster to promote the book and tour, but it would benefit from a little touching up around the eyes. I don't want to completely remove the lines and bags as I feel this would be cheating, but I would like to soften the appearance of the lines to make me look less haggard and more acceptable to the public.

Yours sincerely,
Edwina

Before

Dr. Jackson says...

> **Dear Edwina,**
>
> **By applying the following four simple steps to your photo, you will instantly change your public image from harsh and uninviting to warm and interesting. This will, hopefully, increase sales of your book.**
>
> **Kind regards,**
> **Dr. B. Jackson**

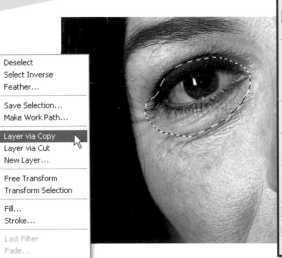

Deselect
Select Inverse
Feather...

Save Selection...
Make Work Path...

Layer via Copy
Layer via Cut
New Layer...

Free Transform
Transform Selection

Fill...
Stroke...

Last Filter
Fade...

1 To begin this quick and easy technique for giving eyes an instant lift, select the Freehand Lasso tool **(L)** from the Toolbox, enter a value of 4 pixels in the Tool Options feather box, and then draw a rough selection around the left eye. When selecting the eye, keep within the crease of overhanging skin above the eye and the deeper lines beneath the eye. Copy the selection to a new layer by pressing **Ctrl/⌘+J** or by right/control-clicking within the selection and choosing Layer Via Copy from the pop-up menu.

2 Press **Ctrl/⌘+T** to apply the Free Transform bounding box to the copied eye. Hold down the **Shift+Ctrl/⌘** keys while dragging the bottom right handle to constrain the eye's proportions as you increase its size slightly. Do not enlarge the eye too much as it will look out of place. Just enlarge it enough to hide the overhanging crease of skin above it.

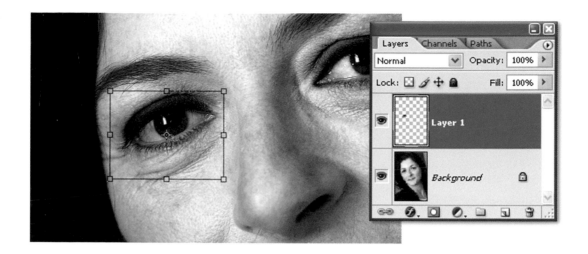

3 Make sure the background layer is activated, then repeat the selection and Free Transform process with the right eye. Once this is done, click on the top layer to activate it and press **Ctrl/⌘+Shift+E** to merge the layers together. Press **(L)** to select the Lasso tool again and draw around the bag below the left eye. Now drag the selection onto the smooth skin of the cheek and press **Alt/⌥+Ctrl/⌘**. Click within the selection to copy the section of skin, and drag the selection back over the eye bag.

4 Go to **Edit > Fade** or press **Ctrl/⌘+Shift+F** to open the Fade dialog box, and drag the slider to the left to reduce the opacity to 60%. Click OK to apply the fade and then **Ctrl/⌘+D** to deselect. By using this technique you have greatly reduced the depth of lines below the eyes without removing them completely, in order to produce a natural-looking result. Now repeat this process with the right eye to complete the eyelift.

After

REMOVING BAGS
Brush away sleep

Before

Dear Dr. Jackson,

If I had the chance to change any part of my body, I would have no hesitation in changing my eyes. When I say eyes, I don't mean the color or shape of my eyes, as I quite like them just as they are. What I do mean is the dark bags beneath them, which make me look constantly tired and haggard. I do what I can with makeup to conceal the dark circles, but if there was some kind of cream or lotion that would banish them permanently I would be happy to try it. Do you know of anything available that can do this, and if so could you recommend it to me?

Yours faithfully,
Denise

Dr. Jackson says...

Dear Denise,

There is only one course of action I can wholeheartedly recommend. I find Photoshop is the perfect product for removing eye bags and balancing uneven skin pigmentation. If you don't believe me, I suggest you follow my five-step plan and see the difference it makes to your appearance. If you are still not convinced, give Michael Jackson a call—he may have some tips on lightening skin.

Kind regards,
Dr. B. Jackson

Patch: ⦿ Source ○ Destination ☐ Transparent

1 Open the image you want to retouch and select the Freehand Lasso tool **(L)** from the toolbox. In the tool options bar, enter a value of 4 pixels in the feather box. Now use the Lasso to make a selection around the lower eye bag and dark shadow beneath the right eye, making sure it contains the whole of the shadow area.

2 Next press the **(J)** key to select the Patch tool from the toolbox, go to the Tool Options bar, and select the source option. Now click within the selection and drag it down to a clean area of skin on the cheek. As you do this, you will see a preview of the destination area at the source point. Release the mouse button and the patch will sample the destination area and seamlessly blend it with the source area, removing the dark shadow.

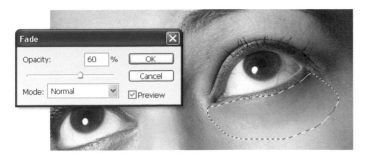

3 Although this process has successfully removed the bag and dark shadow from beneath the eye, it has also removed the skin texture and definition, leaving the patched area looking flat, lifeless, and false. To remedy this, go to **Edit > Fade Patch Selection** or press **Ctrl/⌘+Shift+F** to open the Fade dialog box, and drag the slider to left to lower the opacity of the patch to 60%. This will return some of the original texture and detail. Click OK to apply the fade to the patch and then press **Ctrl/⌘+D** to deselect. Repeat the bag removal process with the left eye.

4 While the fade process has replaced some of the original detail to the area, making the patch more natural, it has also allowed some of the dark shadow to creep back into the image. We will rectify this by adding an adjustment layer to our image. Go to **Layer > New Adjustment Layer > Curves**. When the Curves dialog box appears, adjust the curve to lighten the dark circles beneath the eyes. Do this by dragging the line that runs at a 45° angle across the grid into a lazy S-shape.

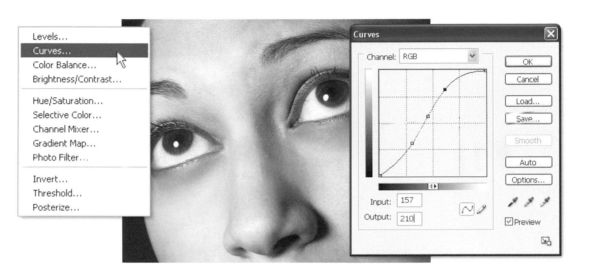

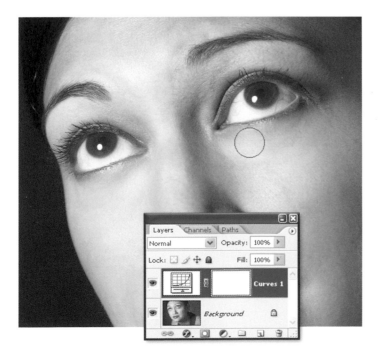

5 Make sure the foreground color is black, then press **Alt/⌥+Backspace/←** to fill the curves mask with black, hiding your adjustment. Now switch the foreground color to white, followed by the **(B)** key to select the Brush tool. Select a soft-edged brush with a low opacity, and gently paint with white below the eyes to gradually remove the mask and lighten the dark shadows. When you are happy with the results, press **Ctrl/⌘+E** to merge the layers and complete the job.

After

EYELIDS
Removing overhanging skin

Dear Dr. Jackson,

As a lady of mature years and experience I'm writing to you in the hope that you can help with a small dilemma. After much deliberation I have decided to spend some of my pension on cosmetic eye surgery. The procedure I've decided on is called a blepharoplasty and entails the removal of eye bags from below the eyes, or overhanging skin from the eyelids. My dilemma is whether to just have the upper bag removed, as this is the worst feature of my face, or whether to also have other procedures done at the same time. I know you may wonder who I'm trying to impress at my age. Well, the answer is that it's for nobody but myself. I have included a photograph and would be much obliged if you could show me how I would look after surgery.

Yours sincerely,

Joan

Dr. Jackson says...

Dear Joan,

I can show you how you would like to look, but whether it's how you will actually look is another matter. Having any form of cosmetic surgery is not a decision to be taken lightly. I can well understand your resolve to do it for yourself, but if I were you I'd save my pension, buy a computer, and follow my techniques to perform as much virtual surgery as you like. Either that or buy a cat and call it Blepharoplasty.

Kind regards,
Dr. B. Jackson

Before

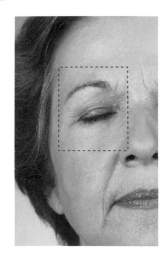

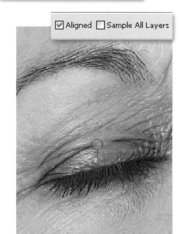

1 Open the image you want to retouch in Photoshop and then hold down **Ctrl/⌘+Space**. As you do this you will notice the cursor changes to the magnify icon. Now click and hold the left mouse button as you drag to create a square selection around the left eye, let go of the mouse button, and the screen will instantly zoom into the selected area.

2 Select the Clone Stamp tool from the Toolbox by pressing the **(S)** key. Go to the Tool Options bar and choose a reasonably small soft-edged brush, set the blend mode to Lighten, and then tick the Aligned box. Now hold down the **Alt/⌥** key and click on the center of the eyelid to select a sample point. Reposition the cursor over the dark-lined edge of the overlapping skin, hold the mouse down, and paint along the line. As the Aligned box has been ticked, the clone sample point will follow the movement of the brush, cloning the eyelid over the flap of skin.

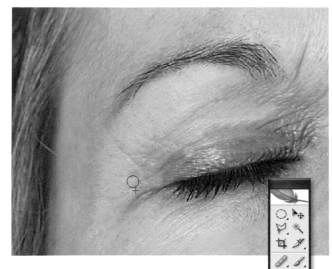

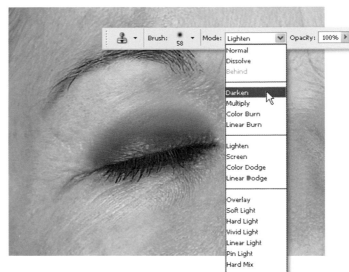

3 Because you are cloning in Lighten mode, the only pixels that will be replaced in the process are those that are darker than the sample point. This makes it ideal for removing dark lines and wrinkles while leaving the skin's highlights in place. Carry on using this process to remove the deeper lines and wrinkles over the eye. Sample as close to the line as possible and always follow the direction of the line.

4 Remember, the aim here is to look as natural as possible, so you need to remove the overhanging skin without removing the original skin texture. If you find the image looking a little patchy, with too many lighter areas, switch the blend mode to Darken. This will then replace only the pixels lighter than the sample point and reduce the lighter patches. Once all the lines are removed, repeat the process with the right eye.

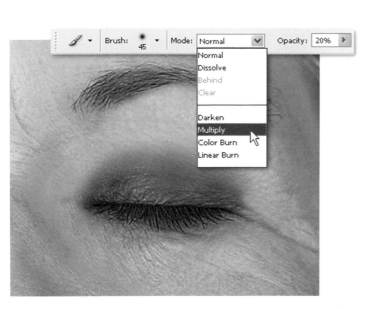

5 Now freshen up the eye makeup. Press **(B)** to select the Brush tool and right/control-click the mouse to bring up the brush picker. Choose a soft-edged brush. Now go to the Tool Options bar, select Multiply from the drop-down blend modes menu, and set the brush opacity to 20%. Hold down the **Alt/** ⌥ key to temporarily bring up the Eyedropper tool and select the color of the eye shadow. Brush over the eyelids a couple of times to touch up the eye shadow.

After

THE NOSE JOB
From aquiline to simply fine

Dear Dr. Barry,

I have recently gone through a messy divorce and now find myself on the wrong side of 40, financially secure, positive, but very lonely. I have been giving serious consideration to joining an Internet dating agency but I'm a little apprehensive about posting a picture of myself on the web. I have quite a large nose and I fear this will put off prospective dates from arranging to meet me. Are there any easy Photoshop techniques you can show me to reduce the size of my nose? I know this may sound a little deceptive, but I'm sure if a good man got to know me he wouldn't be put off by the size of my nose.

Yours faithfully,
Stephanie

Before

Dr. Jackson says...

"**Dear Stephanie,**

My old granddaddy once told me: "If you're gonna go fishing, boy, make sure you use the right bait." So I understand where you are coming from. Try this trouble-free technique and I guarantee you'll be reeling in men for months. Just remember to throw back the ones you don't want.

**Kind regards,
Dr. B. Jackson**"

1 Open the image in Photoshop and make duplicate of the layer (by clicking on Duplicate Layer in the Layers menu). This will allow us to work on a copy of the image without affecting the original. Press **Ctrl/⌘+Shift+X** to open the Liquify filter workspace, then hold down **Ctrl/⌘+Space**, and click and drag the mouse around the nose to quickly zoom into that sizable area.

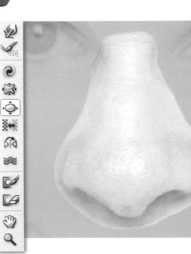

2 Hit the Mask All button from the Mask Options dialog box. This will place a mask over the whole image. (You can change the color of mask in the view options dialog—I have used green in this example.) Select the Thaw Mask tool **(D)** from the tools on the left of the workspace and use it to remove the mask from the nose area. This will allow you to work on the pixels of the nose without affecting the remainder of the image.

3 Now select the Pucker tool **(S)** and set the brush size large enough to cover the whole of the nose area. Position the center of the brush over the tip of the nose and click the mouse. Watch in awe as the nose shrinks before your eyes. To achieve a natural-looking result, use this effect sparingly—with each click of the mouse,

the nose will shrink farther. If you feel you have taken the effect too far, you can go back one stage at a time by pressing the Reconstruct button, or go back to the original to start again by pressing the Restore All button.

4 If the Show Mesh option is checked in the View Options pane, the underlying grid is made visible, which allows you to see clearly where distortion has been applied. This can be saved at any point during transformation by clicking on the Save Mesh button, so it can then be loaded again later to return the transformation to that particular stage. Checking the Show Backdrop option with the opacity set to 50% allows you to see an undistorted preview of the background layer.

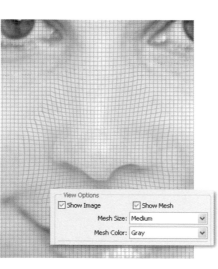

5 When you are happy with the results of the transformation, simply click the OK button to apply the changes to your copy of the original image. Try turning the adjusted layer on and off to fully appreciate the transformation from aquiline to simply fine.

After

NOSE LENGTH
Longer or shorter

Dear Dr. B Jackson,

On a number of occasions lately I've caught my husband looking at other women. When I've confronted him about it he denies it, saying how could he look at another woman when he only has eyes for me? I'm convinced he is lying and I think he is losing interest in me because of my long nose; I've always hated the length of my nose and have thought many times about having it shortened but have never had the nerve. Now, though, I have decided that if it means I can keep my husband interested, then I'll do it. Could you please advise me of a reputable clinic that could carry out my wishes and explain to me the methods involved in such a procedure. You are my last hope of keeping my marriage alive.

Yours faithfully,
Adriana

Dr. Jackson says...

Dear Adriana,

There's an old Chinese proverb that says, "Man who looks at bowl of rice is not always hungry, but man who eats bowl of rice must pay for the pleasure." Roughly translated I think it means you can look, so long as you don't touch, which seems to be the case here. I think you may have convinced yourself that your husband is interested in other women because you hate your nose. I'm sure if your husband has never made an issue of the length of your nose before, there is no reason for him to do so now. I would suggest to you that you apply my simple four-stage procedure to your photographs and show them to your husband to gauge his reaction, but do it quickly just in case I'm wrong and you are right.

Good luck,
Dr. B. Jackson

Before

1 Before using this extremely easy technique to shorten the nose, bear in mind that the shorter you make the nose, the longer the top lip will become. So, unless you want to start rearranging all the features of the face, it is best used in moderation. Begin by pressing the **(L)** key to select the Lasso tool from the Toolbox, and use this to make a rough selection around the nose. Don't be too precise when making the selection, as it is important to retain some of the skin area around the nose, especially the top lip area beneath the nose.

2 Now press **Alt/⌥+Ctrl/⌘+D** (or go to **Select > Feather**) to open the Feather Selection dialog box. Enter a value of 8 pixels as the feather radius, then click OK to apply the feather to the selection. We will now copy the selection onto its own separate layer by pressing **Ctrl/⌘+J**, which will allow us to alter the shape of the nose without affecting the original background layer below.

3 Go to **Edit > Free Transform** (or press **Ctrl/⌘+T**) to apply the Free Transform command bounding box to the selection. Click on the handle at the bottom center of the bounding box and drag upward. As you do, you will see the nose shorten. Drag until you are happy with the new length of the nose, remembering to try to keep it in proportion with the rest of the facial features. Press the **Return/↵** key to apply the change.

4 If, when reducing the nose layer, any of the original nose shows beneath, press the **(S)** key to select the Clone Stamp tool and clone over it with skin sampled from the top lip (making sure the Use All Layers box is ticked in the Tool Options bar). In this example I only shortened the nose slightly to make a subtle difference—this meant I did not have to clone over the original nose as there was enough top lip selected in the new nose layer to easily cover the background. There was, however, an obvious join line below the nose where the skin tones did not match. To remedy this I pressed **(J)** to select the Healing Brush tool, ticked the Use All Layers option, and held down **Alt/⌥** while clicking on an area of skin above the lip to sample it. I then brushed over the join with the Healing Brush to better blend the nose layer with the background. Finally I pressed **Ctrl/⌘+E** to merge the layers.

After

NOSE SLIMMING
Narrower nasal contours

Dear Dr. Jackson,

For many years now I have had a major hang-up about the shape of my nose. The top section of my nose is quite narrow, but as it nears the tip it widens dramatically, giving me a permanent flared nostrils appearance. I think it makes me look like I've been hit in the face with a frying pan. Please could you help me by showing me how to reduce the width of the end of my nose without affecting the top half of it, which I like?

Regards,
Sarah

Dr. Jackson says...

Dear Sarah,

Not only is the following trouble-free method for slimming the nose perfect for frying-pan noses, but it can also just as easily be applied to widen the nose. So, if you know anybody who looks like they have had their nose pinched by pliers, let them know about this, too.

Kind regards,
Dr. B. Jackson

Before

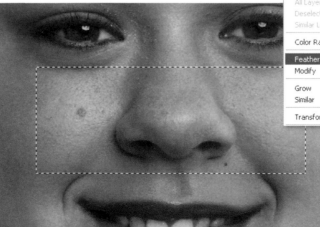
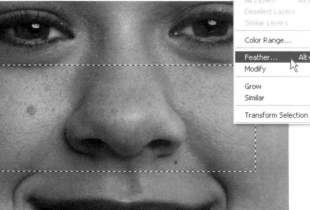

1 After opening the image you want to work on, press the **(M)** key to select the Rectangular Marquee tool. Click on the left cheek and then drag the mouse to the right to create a rectangular selection marquee across both cheeks and the lower half of the nose.

Select	
All	Ctrl+A
Deselect	Ctrl+D
Reselect	Shift+Ctrl+D
Inverse	Shift+Ctrl+I
All Layers	Alt+Ctrl+A
Deselect Layers	
Similar Layers	
Color Range...	
Feather...	Alt+Ctrl+D
Modify	▶
Grow	
Similar	
Transform Selection	

2 Now press **Alt/⌥+Ctrl/⌘+D** (or use the menu option **Select > Feather**) to open the Feather Selection dialog box. Enter a value of 8 pixels as the feather radius, then click OK to apply the feather to the selection. We will now copy the selection onto its own separate layer by pressing **Ctrl/⌘+J**, which will allow us to alter the shape of the nose without affecting the original background layer below.

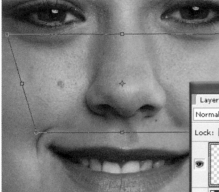

3 Go to **Edit > Free Transform** (or press **Ctrl/⌘+T**) to open the Free Transform command bounding box around the selection. Hold down **Ctrl/⌘+Alt/⌥+Shift** and drag the bottom left handle inward. As you do so, you will see that the bottom right handle also moves inward proportionally, slimming the lower half of the nose. When you are happy with the amount of slimming applied to the nose, press the **Return/↵** key to apply the change.

4 We can now see that, although the width of the nose has been reduced by the required amount, the slimming process has left the cheeks slightly deformed. To remedy this we shall apply a layer mask. Go to **Layers > Add Layer Mask > Hide All** (or hold down the **Alt/⌥** key and click on the mask icon at the bottom of the layers palette). This adds a black-filled layer mask, which hides the slimmed nose layer and shows the original background layer.

5 Press the **(B)** key to select the Brush tool, and choose the soft-edged variety from the Tool Options bar. Press the **(D)** key to make the foreground color white, and gently paint over the nose area to remove the mask and reveal the slimmer version of the nose. If too much of the mask is removed, press the **(X)** key to switch the foreground color to black and paint to reinstate the mask. When happy with results, right/control-click on the layer mask in the Layers palette and choose Apply Layer Mask from the pop-up menu. Finally hit **Ctrl/⌘+E** to merge the layers and view the results of the new slimmer nose.

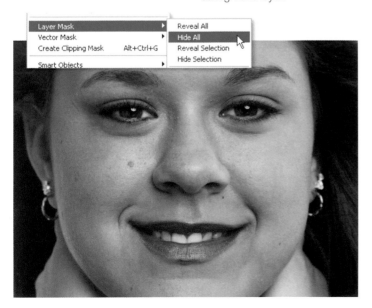

STRAIGHTER NOSE
Nasal narcissism for the neurotic

Dear Dr. B. Jackson,

As you can probably tell from my photograph I used to be an amateur boxer, and although I thoroughly enjoyed the sport, I have to say I was not particularly good at it. After my fifth knockout in a row, and my fourth broken nose, I decided to quit boxing. Not only was it proving to be a danger to my health, but also a major a blow to my self-esteem. Now that I have retired from the game I am contemplating having my nose reset, but would appreciate it if you could first give me some indication of how my nose would look after such a procedure.

Stu

Dr. Jackson says...

Dear Stu,

How does that old saying go? "Where there's no sense, there's no feeling." Well, you obviously had some sense left to get out of your ill-fated boxing career when you did; it's just a shame it took four broken noses to find it. I suggest that now you have come to your senses, make use of them and follow my simple steps to producing a perfectly straight nose. Oh, and take up a less dangerous pastime, such as flower arranging.

Kind regards,
Dr. B. Jackson

Before

1 For this procedure we will be using the versatile Liquify command to make easy work of what, at first glance, may appear to be a difficult task. Start by opening the image you wish to work on and then go to **Filter > Liquify** (or press the keyboard shortcut **Ctrl/⌘+Shift+X**) to open the Liquify command interface.

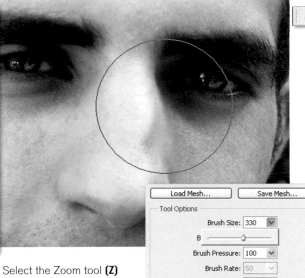

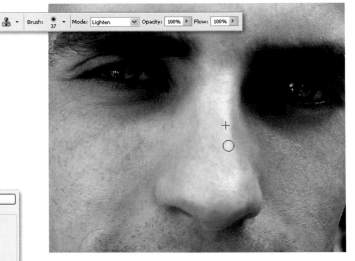

2 Select the Zoom tool **(Z)** from the bottom of the Liquify tool pane, position the cursor over the center of the man's face, and mouse-click a few times to zoom into the nose. Return to the tool pane, this time choosing the Forward Warp tool from the very top of the list of options. In the Tool Options pane, set the brush size to 330 pixels, the brush density to 20, and the brush pressure to 100.

4 Although the nose has now been straightened, a dark shadow on the bridge of the nose still gives the impression that it has a slight bend in it. To rectify this we will use the Clone Stamp tool to remove the shadow. Press the **(S)** key to select the tool from the Toolbox, and then go to the Tool Options bar and set the blend mode to Lighten.

Hold down the **Alt/⌥** key and click on the highlighted area (on the center of the nose) to select a sample point. Then clone over the shadow with the sample area to remove it. Now that the shadow has been removed, we can sit back and appreciate our new nose in all its bump-free glory.

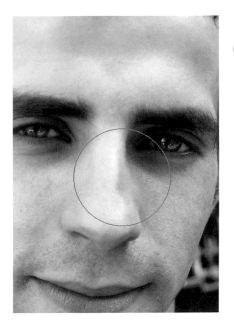

3 Position the center of the brush next to the bump on the nose, then hold down the mouse button and drag the mouse to the left. As you do this, you will see that the image pixels covered by the brush are pushed to the left, which has the effect of flattening the bump, thereby straightening out the nose. When you are happy with the amount of distortion applied to the image, click on the OK button to accept the changes made to the image, and return to the main Photoshop interface.

After

SKIN TREATMENT
Frugal facial care

Before

Dear Dr. Jackson,

Could you recommend to me any of the following skin treatments, to help me regain my once smooth youthful complexion? I have heard of acid skin peels that improve the skin's texture, removing fine lines, wrinkles, and blemishes to produce a smooth, younger-looking skin. I have also heard of a process called microdermabrasion, which mechanically exfoliates the skin to produce a softer, smoother look. As I have a low pain threshold and I'm not very well off financially, I was wondering which of these processes would you recommend as the least painful and the most cost effective?

Yours Faithfully,
Margaret

Dr. Jackson says...

Dear Margaret,

It's a tough decision—do you pay to have your skin taken off by pouring acid all over it, or do you pay to have an electric sander applied to your face to rub the skin off? They both sound more like methods of torture rather than beauty treatments. I think I can do much better than that and show you a pain-free process that will not cost you a cent—providing you already own a computer installed with Adobe Photoshop, that is.

Kind regards,
Dr. B. Jackson

1 After opening the photo you wish to apply softer skin to, press the **Ctrl/⌘+J** keys twice to make two copies of the image. Turn off the top copy by clicking on the eye symbol next to the layer in the Layers palette, then activate the Layer 1 copy by clicking on it.

2 Now go to **Filter > Blur > Gaussian Blur** to open the Gaussian Blur dialog box. Drag the slider to create a blur with a radius of 20 pixels. Click OK to apply the blur and then set the layer's blend mode by choosing Darken from the drop-down menu at the top of the Layers palette.

3 Click on the top layer to activate it and then go to **Filter > Blur > Gaussian Blur**—or simply press **Ctrl/⌘+F**, to apply the same 20-pixel radius blur applied to the last layer to this layer too. Set the blending mode of this layer to Lighten. Then press **Ctrl/⌘+Shift+N** or click on the Create New Layer icon at the bottom of the Layers palette to create a new blank layer.

4 Turn off the background layer by clicking on the eye icon next to it, then hold down the **Alt/⌥** key and click on the arrow at the top-right corner of the Layers palette to open the drop-down layer options menu. While still holding the **Alt/⌥** key, choose the Merge Visible option from the menu to create a flattened version of the previous two layers. Next, turn the background layer back on and Layer 1 and its copy off. Activate Layer 2 by clicking on it, and reduce the opacity of the layer to 50%.

5 We have given the skin a much softer appearance at the expense of details like eyes and teeth. To remedy this, go to the History palette and check the tick box next to the opening image. This sets the image state that the History Brush will paint back to. With the History Brush tool and a soft-edged brush, paint over all the areas that should have detail, such as the eyes, teeth, and hair. Finally, to combine the layers and complete the treatment, click **Layer > Flatten Image**.

After

DIGITAL BOTOX
Smooth away the ravages of time

Doctor,

I desperately need your help, I have recently been asked to submit a current photograph of myself to a national magazine, which would be of great promotional value to my new business. The problem is I have very defined lines on my forehead that make me look like I am permanently frowning. Unfortunately, as I'm sure you can appreciate, this isn't the best look for the director of a new cosmetics company. Is there a simple Photoshop technique you can show me that would reduce the definition in the lines on my forehead without having to resort to botox injections?

Yours in desperation,
Malcolm

Dr. Jackson says...

Dear Malcolm,

I totally understand how problematic your situation is, but don't worry. If you complete the following five fundamental steps to a flawless frown, then you will have no problem pulling the wool over your clients' eyes for many years to come.

With best wishes,
Dr. B. Jackson

Before

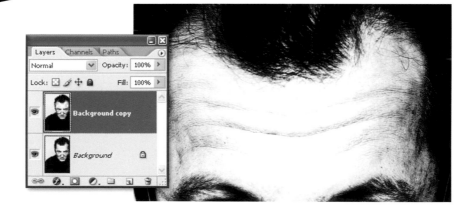

1 Open the image you intend to work on, then immediately duplicate it by dragging the background layer onto the Create New Layer icon at the bottom of the Layers palette. This will make an identical copy of the background layer, entitled "Background copy," that is placed above it on the Layers palette.

2 Select the Healing Brush tool **(J)** from the Toolbox and click on the down arrow next to the brush on the toolbar to open up a dialog box where the brush diameter, hardness, spacing, and shape can be edited.

3 Hold down the **Alt/⌥** key and click to select a sample source point on an area of smooth skin, then click and drag to paint over the wrinkles you wish to remove. Watch as they are miraculously replaced with smooth skin. Repeat this process until all the wrinkles have been removed.

4 Now that the wrinkle removal procedure has been completed, it is plain to see that our digital botox has much in common with the real procedure. The process has left the forehead looking too smooth and lifeless, making the image look too obviously retouched.

5 This is easily remedied by reducing the opacity of the top layer, allowing the more prominent wrinkles from the background layer to show through and create a much more realistic effect. The layers can now be flattened to complete the transformation from tired and old to trendy and bold.

After

REMOVING WRINKLES
Clean away crows' feet

Dear Dr. Jackson,

I would be very grateful if you could you grant me the benefit of your expertise and advise me on the best form of treatment to alleviate the signs of aging, namely the removal of wrinkles and crows' feet from around the eyes. I believe there are a number of anti-aging creams and serums available to purchase and I have also heard there are chemicals that can be injected into the wrinkles to smooth them out. Could you tell me if any of these remedies produce permanent results and which would you recommend, if any? Or perhaps you know of another, more effective form of treatment?

Yours sincerely,

Elizabeth

Dr. Jackson says...

Dear Elizabeth,

As a Photoshop surgeon I'm afraid that I am not qualified to offer you recommendations on products or remedies commercially available. What I can state as fact, though, is that none of the treatments you mention in your letter produce permanent results. Unfortunately, we all fall prey to the ravages of time and nothing we do can ever stop these effects—apart from Dr. Jackson's tried and tested solution to a wrinkle-free face: liberally apply my formula to all your photographs and watch in disbelief as the years literally fade away.

Kind regards,
Dr. B. Jackson

Before

1 The tool traditionally used for removing lines and wrinkles has always been the Clone Stamp tool, and although it is still a very useful tool for this type of work, it has been somewhat superseded by the more intelligent Healing Brush and Patch tools. In this tutorial I will show you examples of both of these tools in action, starting with the Healing Brush.

Open the image you intend to work on and then press the **(J)** key to select the Healing Brush from the Toolbox, right/control-click to bring up the brush options dialog box, and then adjust the sliders to create a soft-edged brush that is slightly wider than the deepest facial lines.

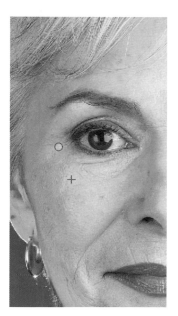

3 Let's turn to the right eye, but this time use the Patch tool. The Patch tool produces much the same results as the Healing Brush, but while that tool works like a brush, replacing the pixels of the area brushed over, the Patch tool creates a selection and replaces the pixels within it. This makes it ideal for correcting larger areas. Press the **(J)** key again to select the Patch tool from the Toolbox. Make sure that the source button is checked in the Tool Options bar and draw a selection around the crows' feet of the right eye. Now simply drag the selection to an area of clear skin and watch as the patch tool magically smoothes out the wrinkles of the selection. Repeat this process until all the wrinkles around the eyes are smoothed out.

2 Hold down the **Alt/⌥** key while clicking on a smooth area of skin close to the wrinkles you want to remove. This samples the texture of the smooth skin, which will then be used to replace the wrinkles. Now hold down the mouse button and simply stroke over the wrinkles. At first the retouch will look obvious, but as soon as you let go of the mouse button, the Healing Brush cleverly blends the new texture with the color and luminosity of the painted area to seamlessly remove the wrinkles. As you can see, spending a couple of minutes using this has produced quite remarkable results.

Brush: 32 | Mode: Normal | Opacity: 30%

Patch: ●Source ○Destination □Transparent

4 As you can now see, the results of this procedure are fantastic, if a little unnatural for a lady of this age. Returning a few lines and wrinkles to the areas around the eyes will produce a far more realistic and natural-looking appearance. To do this press **(Y)** to select the History Brush from the tools palette, and check the History Brush box to the left of the open image in the History palette. This selects the state that the History Brush will paint back from. Set the opacity of the brush to 30% and gently brush around the eyes with a large, soft brush to selectively replace a softer version of the wrinkles.

After

THE PERFECT TAN
Sunkissed without the sunbed

Dear Jane,

I have very pale skin, which means when I go on vacation I have a real problem with the sun. My skin either burns and blisters or I put on so much sun cream to prevent burning that the sun gets nowhere near my skin, leaving me just as pale at the end of the vacation as I was at the beginning. Either way I have never had a natural, healthy-looking tan but would dearly like one. Is there anything you can suggest?

Regards,
Sarah

Before

Nurse J. Peg says...

Dear Sarah,

I'm asked this question all the time: "How do I keep my tan after the summer has gone?" Well, unless you've got lots of money to spend on sunbeds, I say, "Fake it." Just apply my hassle-free technique for the perfect tan to all your holiday snaps and then show your friends what a great tan you got. One word of advice though: Don't see anybody for at least a couple of months after your holiday—you wouldn't want to spoil the illusion!

Regards, Nurse J. Peg

1 Open the image you wish to add a tan to, and then create a new fill layer by clicking **Layer > New Fill Layer > Solid Color**. When the dialog box appears, name the layer "Tan" and click OK—the color picker palette will then appear. Choose a brown tan color from this and then click OK to fill the new layer with the color.

3 To remedy this we need to remove the blended fill layer from the eyes, hair, and surrounding water, and leave it applied only to the skin. As the New Fill Layer automatically opened up with a Layer mask attached to it, this is easily done by pressing the **(B)** key to select the Brush tool and then painting over the hair and background with black to apply the mask. Zoom into the eyes by holding down **Ctrl/⌘+Space** as you click, and drag the mouse to make a selection of the area. Reduce the size of the brush, and carefully paint over the eyes to allow the background layer to show through.

2 Go to the top of the Layers palette and choose Color Burn from the drop-down blending modes menu. Reduce the opacity of the layer to around 40%. As you can see, this has already achieved the effect of an instant tan on the girl, but it has also darkened the rest of the image, including the eyes, hair, and the surrounding water.

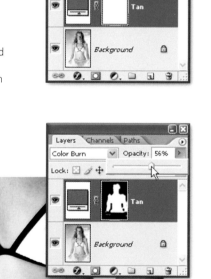

4 Carry on painting with black to apply the mask over the hair and the surrounding water; if you accidentally paint over any of the skin areas, simply paint in white to remove the mask. Now that the fill layer covers only the skin area of the girl, it is easy to darken the tan by increasing the layer opacity, or lightening the tan by decreasing the opacity. For the final result in this example I reduced the opacity to 37% to produce a more natural look, and then pressed **Ctrl/⌘+E** to merge the layers.

After

FRECKLE FADING
Disguising mottled skin

Before

Dear Nurse Jane,

As you can see from my photograph I have bright red hair, which I absolutely love, but I also have a lot of freckles, which I'm not so keen on. Is there any method you could share with me for reducing the appearance of my freckles? I want to send some photos of myself to a modeling agency.

Yours faithfully,

Scarlet

P.S. Is it wrong to alter my pictures before sending them out to agencies?

Nurse J. Peg says...

Dear Scarlet,

If you were to increase the size of your breasts or reduce the size of your bottom before sending your pictures out then that would be wrong. In your case, losing a few freckles may be a touch sneaky, but I wouldn't say it was wrong. After all, these days most models' images are retouched after shooting anyway. To execute your cunning plan, simply apply the following procedure to your entire portfolio and pray they want girls with red hair.

Kind regards,

Jane Peg

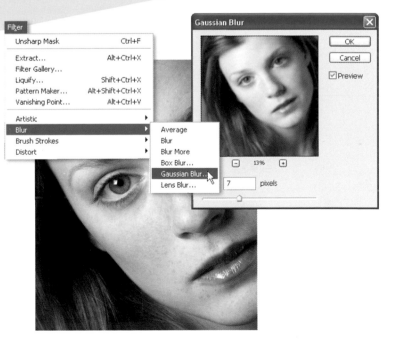

1 Get started by, as always, opening the image you intend to work on into Photoshop. Next, go to **Filter > Blur > Gaussian Blur** to open the Gaussian Blur dialog box. Slide the radius slider to the right until, all the freckles are blurred together and no longer visible; in this example a radius of 7 pixels was enough to achieve the desired effect. Click OK to apply the selected amount of blur to the image.

2 Ensure the History palette is open by clicking on History in the drop-down Windows menu, or by pressing **F9** and then clicking on the History tab at the top of the palette. In the History palette, click on the open box to the left of the second state, which reads Gaussian Blur. By doing this you are setting the state that the History Brush will paint back to. Now click on the first state in the History palette, which reads Open, to return the image to how it looked before the blur filter was added.

3 Select the History Brush tool from the Toolbox by pressing the **(Y)** key, and then go to the Tool Options bar. Choose a soft-edged brush, and from the drop-down blending modes menu, select Lighten. By choosing Lighten mode you are making sure that the History Brush will only replace the pixels that are darker than the blurred state—blurring out the freckles without affecting the lighter parts of the skin.

4 The final stage is to use the History Brush to paint over all the freckles on the face. As you paint you will see the freckles miraculously blend into the skin. If you feel that too much of the skin's detail is being lost, experiment with the opacity of the History Brush until you are happy with the results applied.

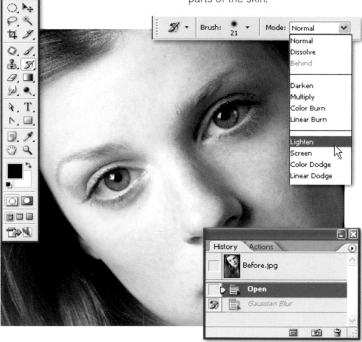

After

HAIR TREATMENT
Bald no more

Dear Dr. Jackson,

I need your help. An old girlfriend of mine recently contacted me through the school reunion website Friends Reunited. It was great to hear from her again after such a long time, so we exchanged addresses. She now e-mails me regularly and I must say I quite look forward to our long-distance chats across the Internet. Yesterday she sent me some recent photographs of herself and she looks fantastic for her age. She has asked me to do the same, but I would be too embarrassed to send her a picture of me as I am now quite bald. My hair, which was always my crowning glory, is very thin and lank and no longer as thick and shiny as it was when she used to run her fingers through it. I would much appreciate it if you could help me with this little problem as I am keen to keep in contact with her, even though I know I will never actually see her again —she now lives in Australia.

Yours faithfully,
Lee

 Dr. Jackson says...

Dear Lee,

I have the perfect hair-restoring treatment for you to apply to any image you would like to send your old girlfriend. The only problem I can foresee is that she may be so impressed with your wonderfully thick head of hair that she will travel all the way from Australia just to run her fingers through it again.

Kind regards,
Dr. B. Jackson

Before

1 After opening the image in Photoshop, press the **(M)** key to choose the Elliptical Marquee tool from the Toolbox. Hold down the left mouse button as you drag out a selection encircling the man's hair. Right/control-click within the selection, or press **Ctrl/⌘+J** to copy the selection to a new layer, and rename the layer "Hair" by double-clicking on it in the Layers palette.

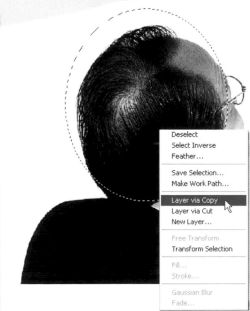

Deselect
Select Inverse
Feather...

Save Selection...
Make Work Path...

Layer via Copy
Layer via Cut
New Layer...

Free Transform
Transform Selection

Fill...
Stroke...

Gaussian Blur
Fade...

2 Now go to **Select > Color Range** to open the Color Range dialog box, set the selection preview to White Matte, and click on the man's hair to select it. Now, drag the Fuzziness slider to the right to increase the selection until all the single strands of hair on the man's head are selected. Click OK to accept the selection, and then press **Ctrl/⌘+Shift+I**, or go to **Select > Inverse,** to invert the selection before hitting **Delete/←**.

Select: 🖋 Sampled Colors

OK Cancel Load... Save...

Fuzziness: 145

☐ Invert

⦿ Selection ○ Image

Selection Preview: White Matte

3 Click on the eye icon to the left side of the background layer to turn it off and you will see that you are left with just the man's hair on the hair layer. Activate the hair layer by clicking on it, then press **Ctrl/⌘+D** to deselect the selection. Now use the Eraser tool **(E)** to tidy up the hair selection and erase the lower, thicker section of hair, leaving just the thinner strands of hair remaining.

Layers Channels Paths

Normal Opacity: 100%

Lock: ☐ 🖌 ✛ 🔒 Fill: 100%

Hair

Background

4 Turn the background layer back on and set the hair layer's blending mode to Darken. Press the **(V)** key to select the Move tool, and then press the left arrow key twice to nudge the hair layer two pixels to the left. As you can see, this instantly thickens the man's hair by filling the gaps between the strands of hair with new hair. Make a copy of the hair layer by dragging it onto the Create New Layer icon at the bottom of the Layers palette, and use the Move tool **(V)** to reposition this layer to fill in more of the gaps on the man's head. Use the Eraser tool **(E)** to remove any sections of hair that stray outside of the hairline, and then repeat this process a number of times until the scalp is completely covered by hair. Finally go to **Layer > Flatten Image** to compress the layers and reveal a natural-looking, thicker head of hair.

Layers Channels Paths

Darken Opacity: 100%

Lock: ☐ 🖌 ✛ 🔒 Fill: 100%

Hair

Background

After

COLORING GRAY HAIR
Blondes do have more fun

Dr. Jackson says...

Dear Dr. Jackson,

I realize I'm in the autumn of my years but I think I look good for my age. The only thing I feel spoils my appearance and makes me look old is my drab gray hair. I certainly wouldn't consider having it dyed; I prefer to grow old gracefully rather than desperately clinging onto my youth. Having said that, a friend recently introduced me to the joys of image manipulation and I've really been enjoying adjusting pictures of myself on the computer. One of the things I've been trying to do but can't get to grips with is returning my hair to its original natural blonde color. Is there a technique you could recommend to help me? I would look great if I still had blonde hair.

Yours faithfully,
Diana

Dear Diana,

Thank you for your letter. Coloring gray hair can be quite tricky as its luminosity and brightness affect any color that you try to blend with it, making it much lighter than you would expect. The Color Replacement tool (as demonstrated on page 68) is very useful for this type of job, but can sometimes leave gray hair looking a little too bright and false. For a more natural look, try the following technique to turn a silver surfer into a blonde bombshell.

Kind regards,
Dr. B. Jackson

Before

1 We will start by making a selection of the hair. Press **(Q)** to enter Quick Mask mode and then **(B)** to select the Brush tool. Make sure the foreground and background colors are set to the default black and white setting by pressing the **(D)** key, and then paint over the hair to apply the mask. When applying the mask, take your time, as the finished result will only be as good as the created mask. Pressing the **(X)** key will change the brush color to white if you need to remove sections of the mask. Pressing the square bracket keys while you paint will increase and decrease the size of the paintbrush.

2 When the mask is complete, press the **(Q)** key again to revert to standard mode; this will make the area outside of the mask a selection. As you require the masked area to be selected, go to **Select > Inverse** (or press **Ctrl/⌘+Shift+I**) to invert the selection. Next press **Ctrl/⌘+J** to copy the selection to a new layer.

3 Go to the Lock section at the top of the Layers palette and click the Lock Transparent Pixels icon. This will enable you to directly paint onto the hair selection without the paint spilling over onto the transparent areas of the layer. Press **(B)** to select the Brush tool and then click on the foreground swatch to bring up the Color Picker. Choose a dark, chocolate-brown color.

4 Set the brush's blend mode to Color in the Tool Options bar and paint over the hair layer. As you are blending the brown paint color onto a light background, it will give you the desired final color—a yellowy blonde. This instantly looks better than the original gray hair color, but loses some of the depth in the darker areas of the hair, making it look a little brassy. To remedy this, simply go to the layers palette and set the hair layer's blending mode to Darken. Merge the layers together by pressing **Ctrl/⌘+E** and view the finished result, a transformation from gray and dowdy to blonde and breezy.

After

RECEDING HAIRLINE
Why the long face?

Dear Dr. Jackson,

I'm looking for any information whatsoever about hair regrowth. I have got a good thick head of hair, but quite a high forehead, which makes me look like I've got a really long face. I'm very self conscious about this as on more than one occasion a work colleague of mine has shouted across the crowded office, "Hey Mike, what's with the long face?" Everybody seems to find this hilarious except me. It has made me painfully shy, especially with women. I've heard there are a few medically proven products on the market that stimulate the hair follicles and promote the regrowth of hair. These products are expensive though, so I was wondering if you could help me with the following questions: How effective are they? Would they make me more attractive?

Yours sincerely,
Mike

Before

Dr. Jackson says...

Dear Mike,

I'm sure you can appreciate that it would be unethical of me to recommend any commercial product that I feel might solve your problem. What I can do is apply an extremely simple but effective, proven formula to your photograph, which will produce your desired effect without scalping you in the process. As for making you more attractive to the opposite sex, I suggest you send the retouched photograph to an online dating agency and wait for the offers to roll in. Just make sure that when you date all those lovely ladies, you keep your baseball cap on.

**Kind regards,
Dr. B. Jackson**

1 This is a very simple procedure, and once you know how it is done, it can be completed in just a few minutes. It does help, though, if the original photograph is taken straight on from the front with a decent amount of hair showing on top, just like the one we're using here. Open your image

and then hold down the **Shift** key while pressing the **(L)** key to scroll through the Lasso tools, and select the Polygonal Lasso tool. Click within the hairline and make a rough selection of the top of the head. Right-click within the selection and choose Layer Via Copy from the pop-up menu.

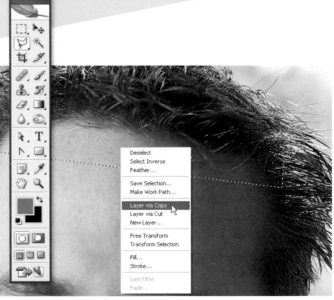

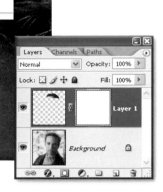

2 Press **Ctrl/⌘+T** or go to **Edit > Free Transform** and the Free Transform bounding box will appear around the selection. Drag the bottom center handle of the bounding box to stretch the selection downward. The amount the selection is stretched will vary for each image, depending on how low on the forehead you want the hairline to be. When you are happy with the amount of downward stretching, drag the center side handles so that the sides of the hair are lined up with those of the background image, and then press the **Return/↵** key to apply the changes.

3 Now go to **Layer > Add Layer Mask Reveal All**, select the Brush tool by pressing **(B)** and right/control-click to open the Brushes palette. Choose a soft-edged brush and paint with black over the forehead (on the scalp layer) to remove the mask and reveal the background image underneath.

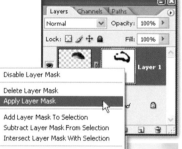

4 Carry on painting with black around the edges of the hair to blend the scalp layer into the background. If too much of the mask is removed, press the **(X)** key to switch the foreground color to white and paint the mask back in. When you are happy with the results of blending the two layers together, right/control-click on the mask icon in the Layers palette and select Apply Layer Mask from the pop-up menu. Finally, press **Ctrl/⌘+E** to merge the layers. Our finished image proves that applying a simple procedure, such as lowering the hairline just a little bit, can not only take away years but also add a good deal of smoldering sex appeal.

After

HAIR IMPLANTS
Scalp surgery simulation

Dear Photoshop Doc,

After many years of trying to hide my balding pate by combing over the few remaining strands of hair I have left, I have decided to bite the bullet and have hair implanted into my scalp. I have been to see a specialist, who has given me all the information about my forthcoming procedure, but the one thing I would have liked that he could not provide me with is a photographic projection of the end result. Do you think it would be possible for you to show me how I would look with a full head of natural hair?

Yours faithfully,

Alan

Dr. Jackson says...

Dear Alan,

If you follow my simple technique of copying and repositioning sections of existing hair, you will be able to build up a full head of hair in no time at all. I'm afraid the real procedure will not be quite as quick and it may leave your head looking like it has been used as a dartboard for a while—but don't worry, because I'm sure it won't look any worse than your tie.

Best of luck,
Dr B. Jackson

Before

Expand Selection

Expand By: 4 pixels

OK
Cancel

1 After opening the image in Photoshop, press the **(W)** key to select the Magic Wand tool and then click on the white background to turn it into a selection. Go to **Select > Modify > Expand**, enter a value of four pixels in the Expand dialog box, and then go to **Select > Inverse** (or press **Ctrl/⌘+Shift+I**) to switch the selection from the background to the man. Copy the selection to a new layer by pressing **Ctrl/⌘+J** and then switch off the background layer by clicking on the eye icon next to the layer in the Layers palette.

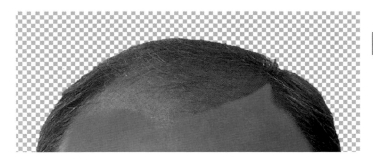

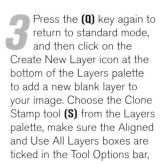

2 Press the **(Q)** key to enter Quick Mask mode, followed by the **(D)** key to ensure the default black and white foreground/background colors are selected. Now press the **(B)** key to select the Brush tool from the Toolbox, and paint with black to create a quick mask across the man's forehead. Imagine

the hairline you would like the man to have and paint the edge of the mask to represent that imaginary hairline. If you need to remove any part of the mask, simply press the **(X)** key to switch the foreground color to white and paint over the mask to remove it.

3 Press the **(Q)** key again to return to standard mode, and then click on the Create New Layer icon at the bottom of the Layers palette to add a new blank layer to your image. Choose the Clone Stamp tool **(S)** from the Layers palette, make sure the Aligned and Use All Layers boxes are ticked in the Tool Options bar,

then hold the **Alt/⌥** key and click on the hair just to the left of the parting. Drag from right to left in an arc across the head to clone the existing hair. Continue cloning the original hair until the forehead is covered to the new hairline (precision isn't too important).

4 As the cloned hair has been placed onto a new layer, it does not affect the original image and can be easily edited with the Eraser. It is now time to add some detail to the hair. Switch off the cloned hair layer for a moment and return to the main layer. Press the **(L)** key to select the Lasso tool and make a selection of the existing hair. Click within the selection and choose Layer Via Copy from the pop-up menu. Position the layer above the cloned hair layer.

5 Use the Free Transform tool to resize and reposition the section of hair, and the Eraser tool **(E)** to blend the edges with the layer beneath. Duplicate the hair section by dragging the layer onto the new layer icon at the bottom of the Layers palette, and repeat the previous Free Transform and blending technique with this section of hair. Carry on repeating this procedure to build up layers of hair from the back of the

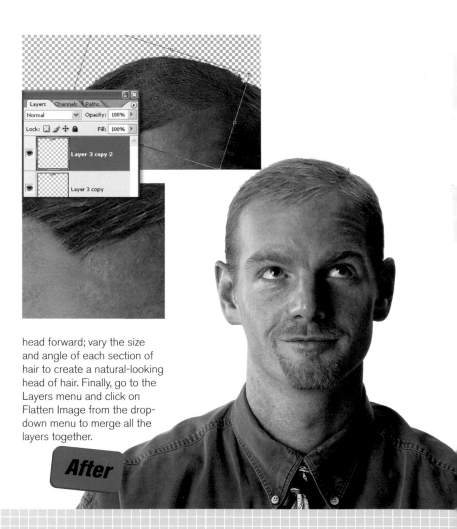

head forward; vary the size and angle of each section of hair to create a natural-looking head of hair. Finally, go to the Layers menu and click on Flatten Image from the drop-down menu to merge all the layers together.

After

WIGS

Artificial artificial hair

Dr. Jackson says...

Dear Dr. Jackson,

As you can see I am completely bald, a total slaphead, as bald as a coot. There's no getting away from the fact that I have absolutely no hair on my head at all and I'm really quite happy about that fact. I have never missed having hair or had the desire to try and recreate how I looked in my youth by having implants or wearing a hairpiece, but I do think it would be fun to see on photographs just how I would look if I still had hair. Could you show me any ways of adding different hairstyles to a photograph of myself without them looking obviously false?

Kind regards,

Ed

Dear Ed,

Montage techniques whereby you add selected parts of one image to another are great fun to do, and, given a little time and effort, easy to master. By following my four-part process to creating perfect wigs, not only will you be learning the basic procedure of creating montages, but you will also be having a lot of fun seeing yourself with various hairstyles. Just remember the mullet was never a good look.

Kind regards,
Dr. B. Jackson

Before

1 This technique of borrowing hair from one image to apply to another relies on both images being shot from the same angle. In this example, both head shots are taken face on with a similar background, which also helps to simplify the process. After opening both the head shots, we will start by extracting the hair from the young man. Go to **Filter > Extract** or press **Alt/⌥+Ctrl/⌘+X** to open up the Extract command interface. Zoom into the hair and then click on the Edge Highlighter tool **(B)** and set the brush size to 12 pixels. Use the Edge Highlighter tool to draw around the edges of the hair, making sure to overlap the hair and the background. Carry on tracing the hairline until all the hair is outlined.

2 Now select the Fill tool **(G)** and click inside the outline to fill it; this adds a blue mask over the hair. Click on the Preview button to view the extraction and use the Edge Touchup tool **(T)** and the Cleanup tool **(C)** to tidy up the edges of the extraction. When happy with the results, press OK. If any further adjustment to the extraction is required, use the History Brush **(Y)** to paint back any sections of the image that were accidentally removed or the Eraser tool **(E)** to remove any unwanted remnants.

Now you know the basic technique for creating wigs, you can have lots of fun experimenting with different styles.

3 Restore down the image window so that both images can be seen on the screen, select the Move tool **(V)**, and drag the hair layer onto the bald man image. Press **Ctrl/⌘+T** (or go to **Edit > Free Transform**) to select the Free Transform tool, and position the hair to fit the head. Now create a Layer mask by going to **Layer > Add Layer Mask > Reveal All**, reduce the opacity of the hair layer to 50% so that the ears can be seen below, and paint with black to remove the hair covering the ears.

Example 2

4 Apply the Layer Mask by going to **Layer > Remove Layer Mask > Apply** and then use the Burn tool **(O)** to darken the hair on the right side of the head, especially where it meets the skin; this will help in achieving a more realistic appearance. When you are happy with the final result, the layers can be flattened by pressing **Ctrl/Cmd+E**.

	Dodge Tool	○
■	Burn Tool	○
	Sponge Tool	○

After

CONTENTS

SECTION 4

Body Beautiful

Dr. Jackson's liposuction plan for painlessly creating the perfect body we all deserve

BREAST ENLARGEMENT
Mammary multiplication

Before

Dear Dr. Jackson,

My boyfriend keeps pestering me to have a boob job; he says he loves me but would love me even more if I had larger breasts. The thing is I'm a little apprehensive about how I would look with bigger boobs. I think I would like them to be a little bit larger but I'm scared that I would end up looking false and ridiculous. Is there any way you can show me in Photoshop what I would look like with larger boobs before I go ahead with any surgery? I am a B cup in size but I think my boyfriend would like me to be at least a D. Can you help?

Marie

Dr. Jackson says...

Dear Marie,

I suggest you follow my painless six-step prescription for larger, natural-looking breasts on a photo of yourself. Show your boyfriend the end result so he can see what he is missing, and then dump the creep. Get yourself a new boyfriend who will love you just the way you are.

Kind regards,
Dr. B. Jackson

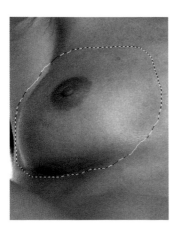

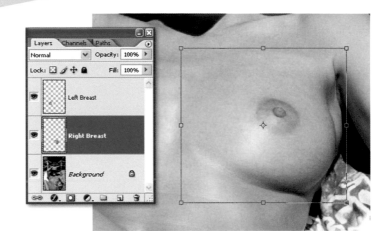

1 After opening your image in Photoshop, press **(L)** to select the Lasso tool, feather by four pixels in the Tool Options bar, and then roughly draw around the left breast to make a selection. Right/control-click on the selection and pick Layer Via Copy from the drop-down menu to copy the selection to a new layer. (Alternatively, press **Ctrl/⌘+C** to copy and **Ctrl/⌘+V** to paste to the new layer.) Select **Layer > Layer Properties** from the menu, and rename the layer "Left Breast." Repeat this process with the right breast.

2 While you are still on the Right Breast layer, select **Transform > Scale** from the Edit menu, hold down **Ctrl/⌘+Shift** to constrain proportions, and drag the bounding box from the top left corner handle. Enlarge the breast by 20% or so, as shown in the Tool Options bar, then double-click the selection (or press **Return/↵**) to apply the change. Repeat this process with the left breast.

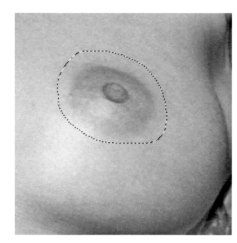

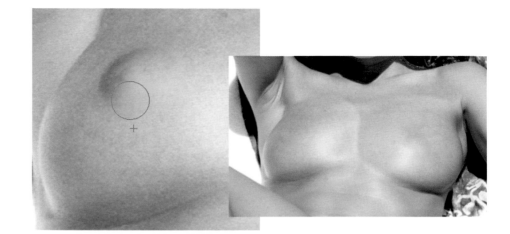

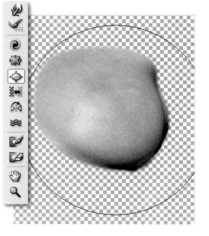

3 We will now make a copy of each nipple before we use the Liquify tool. Press **(L)** to select the Lasso tool, feather by four pixels (again, set this with the Tool Options bar), and then roughly draw around each nipple in turn. Copy each nipple to a separate layer as per step one, then name them "Right nipple" and "Left nipple."

4 Turn off the new nipple layers by clicking on the eye icon to the left of each layer's entry in the Layers palette. We will now use the Clone Stamp tool **(S)** to copy sample areas of each breast over the nipples on the breast layers. Position the cursor over a plain area of the breast, hold down the **Alt/⌥** key to select the sample, move the cursor over the nipple, and click the mouse to clone the sample area over the nipple.

5 With the breasts now nipple-less, select Liquify from the drop-down Filter menu. This will open the breast layer within the Liquify filter workspace. Select the Bloat tool **(B)** from the tool palette on the left side, set the brush size to 600, position the cursor over the breast, and click to expand. The Bloat tool magnifies pixels, so to avoid the image looking too distorted, use this effect sparingly. When happy with the results, click on the OK button to apply the change. Repeat the process with the other breast layer.

6 Use the Move tool **(V)** to reposition each breast and then carefully use a soft-edged Eraser **(E)** to remove any unwanted areas from around each breast. The copied nipples can now be applied and re-positioned. Use the soft-edged Eraser again to tidy up around the nipples and then, when you are completely satisfied with the results, select Flatten Image from the Layer menu to compress the layers. The final result is a painless transition from a B to a natural-looking D-cup.

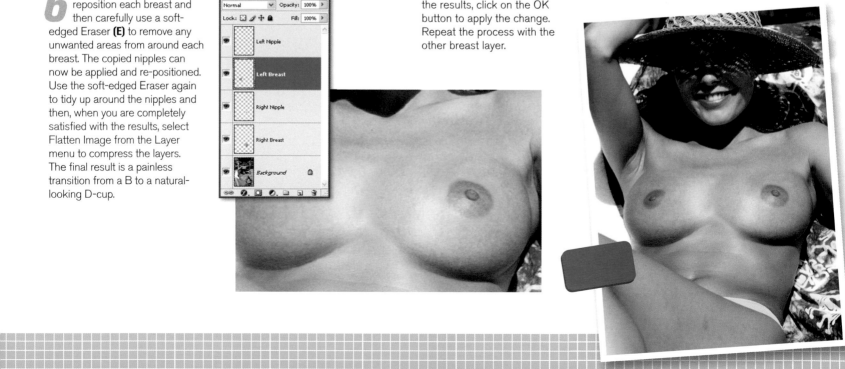

BREAST REDUCTION
Asset management

Dear Dr. B. Jackson,

I'm sure as a man you will find it difficult to understand my problem, but I hope as a doctor you can impartially advise me as to an appropriate course of action. My problem is my breasts: they are too big, they make me look top heavy, they get in the way, and buying clothes to fit both my slim waist and large breasts is a nightmare—and that's not to mention the leering looks and sexist comments I get from men. Life would be so much simpler for me if I had smaller breasts. I could wear a bikini on holiday without feeling like I was one of the attractions in some Victorian peep show. I would be most grateful if you could give me the benefit of your knowledge in this area to advise me on a suitable course of action.

Yours faithfully,

Diana

Before

Dr. Jackson says...

Dear Diana,

You are quite right in your assumption that as a man I would not understand your problem! So my advice is to first complete the following steps to create a smaller bust, so that you can compare before and after shots to help you decide on whether or not to go ahead. Then I suggest you give up this crazy idea and truly appreciate the magnificent gift that nature has bestowed upon you. After all, wasn't it that famous Victorian, Oscar Wilde, who once said, "The only thing worse than being talked about is not being talked about." Think about it!

Dr. Jackson

1 This method for the reducing the size of breasts is very similar to the previous method for enlarging them, but in reverse. After opening the image you want to work on, select the Elliptical Marquee tool **(M)** from the Toolbox, position the cursor over the center of the left breast, hold down **Alt/⌥+Shift**, and drag the mouse to create a circular selection of the left breast. Press **Ctrl/⌘+J** to copy the selection to a new layer and then double click on the new layer in the Layers palette to rename it "Left breast."

2 Return to the background layer by clicking on it in the Layers palette, then repeat the step one selection process with the right breast. Copy this to a new layer by pressing **Ctrl/⌘+J** again and rename that layer "Right breast." Now you have both breasts on separate layers you can turn your attention to resizing them.

3 Return to the left breast layer by clicking on it in the Layers palette, and then go to **Edit > Free Transform** (or press **Ctrl/⌘+T**) to apply the Free Transform bounding box to the left breast. Hold down the **Shift** key as you drag the top right-hand corner handle diagonally inward to resize the breast proportionally. When you are happy with the new size, and while still in Free Transform mode, reposition the breast so that the bikini strap and the side of the body match up with the background. Press **Return/↵** to apply the changes.

4 Repeat the resizing process with the right breast, making sure to keep the breasts in proportion. Afterward, work is needed to blend them back into the original. We will start by first replacing the string between the bikini cups. Turn off the two breast layers by clicking on the eye icon beside each layer and then click on the background layer to activate it. Select the Polygonal Lasso **(L)** from the Toolbox and make a selection of the bikini string. Press **Ctrl/⌘+J** to copy this to a new layer and position this above the two breast layers in the Toolbox.

5 Turn the breast layers back on and use Free Transform to reposition and stretch the bikini string to fit the new resized breasts. Click on the eye icon to turn off the background layer then press **Ctrl/⌘+Shift+E** to combine the two breast layers with the string layer. The tops of the new breasts can now be blended with the background image by clicking on the Add Layer Mask icon at the bottom of the Layers palette, which will apply an editable layer mask to the image.

6 Paint the mask above the breasts with a soft black brush to blend the new breasts into the background image, but do not paint the mask below the breasts, as this will only reveal more of the larger breasts beneath. When happy with the results, apply the layer mask by going to **Layer > Remove Layer Mask > Apply** and then merge the two layers together by pressing **Ctrl/⌘+E**. Select the Clone Stamp tool by pressing the **(S)** key and then take your time to clone the skin from the stomach and chest areas over the obvious join between the two layers, completing the transformation from big and bouncy to petite and pert.

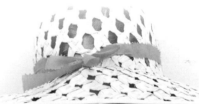

After

BREAST LIFT
Luscious lift

Before

Dear Photoshop Doctor,

I used to be really quite proud of my breasts. They were nice and firm and very pert, but after having two children and breast-feeding them both, I have to say they are not as perky as they used to be. This has left me feeling a little bit self-conscious about my sagging breasts, and I would no longer dream of going topless on the beach, which was something I always loved to do. I won't even let my husband see me without a bra on anymore because I am so embarrassed by them.

I would be much obliged if you could help me with this problem before my breasts go even further south, along with my self-esteem.

Yours faithfully,
Beth

Dr. Jackson says...

Dear Beth,

It sounds to me like you need your spirits lifting, as well as your breasts, and luckily for you I could be just the person to do that. Simply follow my fundamental procedure for producing perfectly pert puppies and you will be so impressed with the results you will be back to flashing your boobs again in no time.

Good luck,
Dr. B. Jackson

1 After opening the image in Photoshop, immediately duplicate it by dragging the layer onto the Create New Layer icon at the bottom of the Layers palette. Next we will use the Elliptical Marquee tool **(M)** to select the right nipple, and paste it onto is own layer by right/control-clicking within the selection and choosing Layer Via Copy from the pop-up menu. Repeat with the left nipple to place that on a separate layer also.

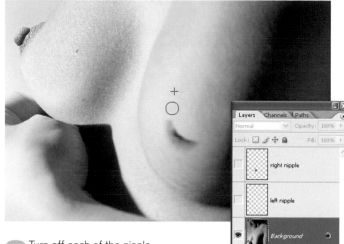

2 Turn off each of the nipple layers by clicking on the eye icon next to them in the Layers palette. Make the background layer active by clicking on it, then press the **(S)** key to select the Clone Stamp tool from the Toolbox. Hold down the **Alt/⌥** key to select a skin sample close to the right nipple, and then clone the sample area of skin over the nipple using a soft-edged brush. Regularly resample the skin around the nipple to ensure the tone and texture of the skin match, and then repeat the cloning technique to remove the left nipple.

3 Now that both nipples have been removed and saved to separate layers, you can begin the process of lifting the breasts without distorting the shape of the nipples. Press **Ctrl/⌘+Shift+X** to enter the Liquify interface and select the Forward Warp tool **(W)** from the tool palette. Set the brush size to 550 pixels, then position the Forward Warp tool over each breast and drag upward to reshape them one at a time. If you would like to compare the distortion with the original image, tick the Show Backdrop box and set the opacity to 50% to show a preview of any distortions made.

4 When you are happy with the new shape of each breast, click the OK button to apply the distortions and return to the main Photoshop interface. Now all you need to do to complete the image is replace and reposition each nipple. Turn each of the nipple layers back on and use the Move tool **(V)** to reposition the nipples on the newly reshaped breasts. The left nipple may need turning slightly to fit, so press **Ctrl/⌘+T** to apply the Free Transform bounding box. Move the pointer outside of the bounding box border and you will see it become a curved, two-sided arrow—drag the mouse up or down to rotate the nipple. Use a soft-edged Eraser tool **(E)** to blend the edges of nipple with the background and then go to the **Layers > Flatten Image** from the drop-down menu to combine all the layers together.

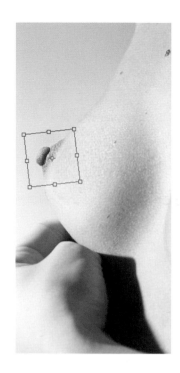

After

THE TUMMY TUCK
Curbing corpulence

Dear Dr. Jackson,

Although I'm in my seventies I'm far more energetic than a lot of men half my age. I have a lot of active interests, including walking, cycling, and windsurfing, as well as photography. I eat lots of fruit and vegetables and generally take good care of my body through leading a healthy lifestyle. My one vice is wine. There is nothing I enjoy more than a nice large glass of quality red wine, and I'm afraid nearly 60 years of taking my favorite tipple has had a lasting effect on my stomach. I'm past the age of worrying about this and I'm certainly not going to give up my favorite drink purely for the sake of a slimmer figure, but it would be nice if you could show me a quick Photoshop method of reducing my flab so that I can impress the ladies in my walking club with my windsurfing photographs.

Yours faithfully,

William

Before

Dr. Jackson says...

Dear William,

Follow my extremely quick and easy four-step procedure for turning flab into firm muscle and I'm sure the ladies of the walking club will be eager to see just how active you really are.

Regards,

Dr. B. Jackson

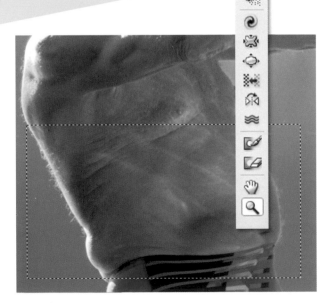

1 Open the image you want to retouch and then go to **Filter > Liquify** or press **Ctrl/⌘+Shift+X** to open the Liquify command interface. Now select the Zoom tool **(Z)** from the tool bar on the left side of the interface. Click and drag out a selection across the man's stomach to give a close-up view, which will also allow greater accuracy when performing the tummy tuck.

2 Next press the **(0)** key to select the Push Pixels Left tool from the toolbar—this can be found sixth down from the top. Now, go to the Tool Options pane and select a brush size of approximately 200 pixels. Position the cursor adjacent to the man's shorts on the right side of his body, and click and drag the mouse upward with one smooth stroke. As you do this, pixels are pushed left, back into the body—instantly slimming the stomach.

Tool Options

Brush Size:	200
Brush Density:	50
Brush Pressure:	50
Brush Rate:	80
Turbulent Jitter:	50
Reconstruct Mode:	Revert

☐ Stylus Pressure

3 Return to the Tool Options palette and reduce the brush size to 100 pixels. Now position the cursor adjacent to the left side of the body, but this time drag the mouse smoothly down to remove the man's love handle. As the Push Pixels Left tool does exactly that, it is important to remember to push or pull it in the right direction for each side of the man. If you were to drag the tool upward on his left side, for instance, it would push the pixels outward, making him fatter rather than thinner.

4 To see a preview layer of the changes made to the image against the original image, tick the Show Backdrop box in the View Options pane, select Blend from the Mode menu and reduce the opacity to 60%. Once you are happy with the slimming results, click on the OK button to apply the changes to the original image and complete the transformation from flabby to firm.

View Options

☑ Show Image   ☐ Show Mesh

Mesh Size: Medium

Mesh Color: Gray

☑ Show Mask

Mask Color: Green

☑ Show Backdrop

Use: All Layers

Mode: Blend

Opacity: 60

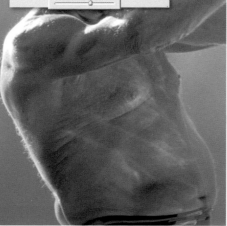

After

BOTTOM RESHAPING
Does my bum look big in this?

Dear Dr. Jackson,

My husband and I were recently looking through a batch of photos taken on our last summer vacation. One in particular caught my attention; it was of me walking along the beach with my back to the camera. I stupidly asked my husband if my bottom looked big in the picture. To my surprise, not only did he reply that it did, but then went on to say I should do more exercise instead of sitting at the computer drinking coffee and eating donuts. Should I:

(a) Take his advice, do more exercise, and diet?
(b) Edit all my holiday photos in Photoshop?
(c) Divorce my husband?

Yours sincerely,
Julie

Dr. Jackson says...

Dear Julie,

Ask your husband to fix you up some coffee and donuts. Eat them when you're busy sitting at the computer, following my simple six-stage plan for producing a slimmer bottom.

With kind regards,
Dr. B. Jackson

Before

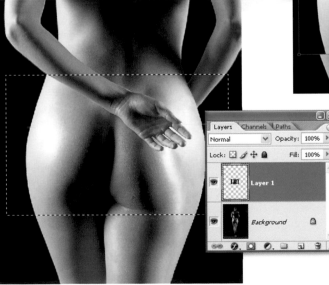

1 This technique works best on a straight-on shot taken from behind, with the model against a plain background. Select the Rectangular Marquee tool **(M)**, hold down the left mouse button, and drag the mouse to create a rectangular selection across the model's bottom. Press **Ctrl/⌘+J** to copy the selection to a new layer.

2 Press **Ctrl/⌘+T** to select the Free Transform tool. Hold down the **Alt/⌥** key to constrain the distortion symmetrically around the center of the selection and drag the handle on the right side inward. As you can see, this instantly slims the bottom, but leaves obvious inward steps from the back and thighs. Hit the **Return/↵** key to accept the change.

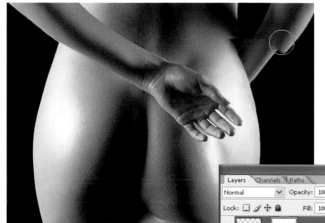

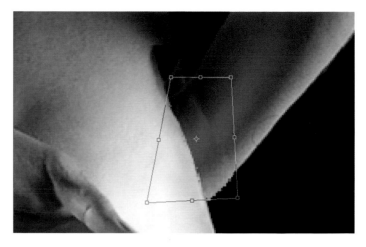

3 Select **Add Layer Mask > Reveal All** from the Layer menu, reduce the flow on the Brush tool **(B)** to 15%, and paint with black over the edges of the layer to gradually reveal the layer underneath. If you remove too much of the layer, paint with white to replace the layer detail. The layer mask can be turned on and off by holding down the **Shift** key and clicking on the layer mask icon. When the two layers are blended together, right/control-click the layer mask icon and select Apply Layer Mask from the drop-down menu.

4 Using the Magnetic Lasso tool, click and draw around the section of arm still attached to the hip. Press **Ctrl/⌘+J** to copy this selection to a new layer. Select **Edit > Transform >**

Distort and drag the corners of the bounding box to make the section of arm fit the gap between the forearm and hip. Flatten the layers and tidy up with the Clone Stamp tool **(S)**.

5 To smooth the stepped areas, press **(P)** to select the Pen tool. It will open with the filled shape layer as the default—in this case the selected color in the Tool Options bar needs to be black. Click on the outline of the girl's waist to create a path, adding anchor points as you go. If you hold down the mouse button as you drag the mouse, the path will begin to curve and two adjustment handles will appear from the anchor point. As you continue the path along the arm, you will notice that a black-filled mask is created between the start and finish points of the path. When you're happy with the created shape, right-click on the shape layer and click on Rasterize Layer to convert the path into a fixed shape.

6 Repeat the previous Pen tool procedure to remove the stepped sections on each leg. Continue the path along the leg to ensure you create a smooth outline. Finally, flatten the layers to complete the transition from large-bottomed girl to lithe supermodel.

After

BOTTOM FIRMING
Chunky cheeks eliminated

Before

Dear Doctor,

For many years I've been perfectly happy passing the time by relaxing on the couch with a good book. My doctor, however, has told me that if I want to live a longer life, I should get off my wobbly behind and take up exercise-cycling perhaps. I'm a bit worried though. I'm not sure that I'll like the look of myself, especially my bottom, afterward. What I want to know, I suppose, is will it still be comfortable, and more to the point, how will it look?

Yours faithfully,
Angela

Dr. Jackson says...

Dear Angela,

I shouldn't worry at all. The kind of tight, firm cheeks you should get from good exercise will still be just as good for sitting on. In fact a bit of muscle mass will do you a power of good when you're sitting on the bicycle's uncomfortable saddle.

Best of luck,
Dr. B. Jackson

Brush: 38 | Mode: Darken | Opacity: 79% | Flow: 100% | Aligned | Sample All Layers

1 We will start by smoothing out the skin on the bottom to remove any spots, stretch marks, or dimples. Press the **(S)** key to select the Clone Stamp tool, go to the options bar, and set the opacity to around 80%. Hold down the **Alt/⌥** key and click on a smooth area of skin close to each imperfection to select a sample, then clone over any lighter imperfections with the Mode option set to Darken. Clone over any darker imperfections with the Mode option set to Lighten.

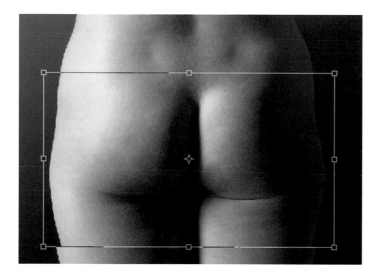

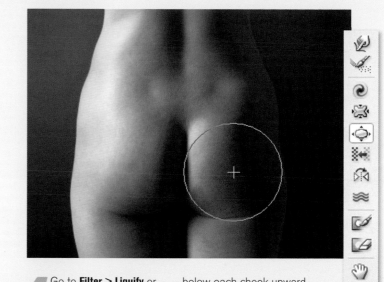

2 Once all the blemishes and imperfections have been removed, select the Rectangular Marquee tool **(M)** from the Toolbox and drag across the image to make a rectangular selection, starting at the base of the back down to the bottom of the picture.

Now press **Ctrl/⌘+J** to copy the selection onto a new layer and then go to **Edit > Free Transform** (or press **Ctrl/⌘+T**) to apply the Free Transform bounding box to the new layer. Drag the center bottom handle upward to remove the sag from the bottom by shortening it.

4 Go to **Filter > Liquify** or press **Ctrl/⌘+Shift+X** to bring up the Liquify interface. Use the Bloat tool **(B)** to slightly expand each bottom cheek and use the Forward Warp tool **(W)** to push the ends of the creases

below each cheek upward to create a more rounded appearance. When satisfied with the applied distortions, click OK to commit the changes to the image and then press **Ctrl/⌘+E** to merge the layers and complete the image.

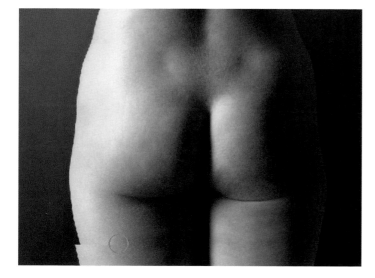

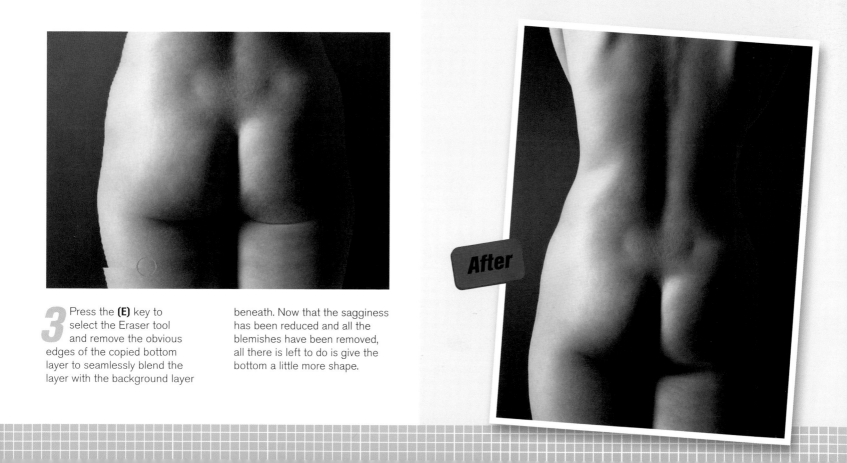

After

3 Press the **(E)** key to select the Eraser tool and remove the obvious edges of the copied bottom layer to seamlessly blend the layer with the background layer

beneath. Now that the sagginess has been reduced and all the blemishes have been removed, all there is left to do is give the bottom a little more shape.

SLIMMER WAIST AND HIPS

Victorian vixens

Dear Doctor Jackson,

I have always thought it would be amazing to have a really tiny waist just like women used to have in the Victorian era. I have tried to recreate the wasp-waisted look on myself but with little success. I tried dieting but this didn't work as not only did I lose weight from my waist but I lost it from my bottom and bust, so I did not achieve the hourglass figure I desired. I have also tried wearing tight-fitting corsets, but found these far too restrictive and uncomfortable to wear for extended periods of time. Would it be possible for you to suggest to me a way of achieving the look I desire, or have women's bodies developed in such a way that this look is no longer achievable?

Yours faithfully,
Samantha

Dr. Jackson says...

Dear Samantha,

It is true that the shape of women's bodies has changed somewhat, but it is also true that Victorian women conditioned their bodies from a young age by squashing them into tight corsets. Because of this many Victorian women suffered problems, such as compression of the intestines or straightening of the spine. Some even died in agony after piercing their liver with their own ribs. I think it may be wiser to simply follow my strategy for achieving a tiny waist without the slow, agonizing death.

Dr. B. Jackson

1 After opening the image in Photoshop, immediately duplicate it by going to **Layer > Duplicate Layer** or dragging the background layer onto the Create New Layer icon at the bottom of the Layers palette. This will enable you to distort the copy layer without disturbing the original background layer beneath.

2 Next, go to **Filter > Liquify** or press **Ctrl/⌘+Shift+X** to open the Liquify command interface. Choose the Forward Warp tool **(W)** from the tool palette and set the brush size to around 460 pixels by clicking on the Brush Size tab and dragging the slider to the right to increase its size. Position the cursor over the right hip and gently drag the mouse to the left to pull the waist inward. Repeat the dragging process with the left hip, pulling the waist inward until you are happy with the new size. Tick the Show Backdrop box. Set the mode to Blend and the opacity to 50% in order to preview the distortions against the original image.

3 When you are happy with the Liquify results, click on OK to apply the distortion and return to the main Photoshop interface. Although the distortions applied to the waist and hips have made them noticeably slimmer, they have also deformed the background. To rectify this, hold down the **Shift** key and repeatedly press the **(L)** key until the Magnetic Lasso tool is selected. Now click on the left side edge of the woman's torso to create a start point, and drag the mouse along the outline of the woman's newly reshaped waist. As you do this, the selection border automatically snaps to the woman's outline. Temporarily switch to the Freehand Lasso to cut across the back by holding down the **Alt/⌥** key while dragging with the mouse button depressed.

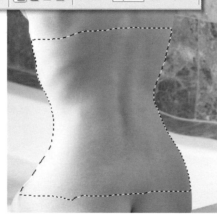

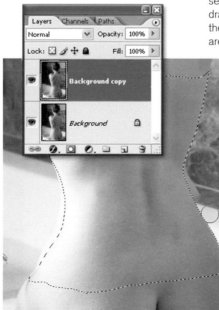

4 Return to the start point to close the selection, and press **Ctrl/⌘+Shift+I** to invert the selection. Now hit the **Delete** key to remove the selected area; you will now be able to see the original undistorted waistline beneath the selection. Activate the background copy by clicking on it in the Layers palette, and with the selection still in place, select the Clone Stamp tool **(S)** from the Toolbox. Hold down the **Alt/⌥** key and click on the bath at the right side of the waist to select a sample point. Carefully drag the mouse to the left until the cursor is above the unwanted area of skin, then click and drag the mouse upward to clone the bath and tiles over the unwanted areas of waistline. To complete the transformation, press **Ctrl/⌘+D** to deselect, followed by **Ctrl/⌘ +E** to merge the layers together.

THINNER THIGHS
Taming thunder thighs

Dear Dr. Jackson,

There is nothing I enjoy more than getting dressed up on a Saturday night and going out clubbing with my girlfriends. We all look ultra sexy and turn heads wherever we go. We rarely spend any money as guys are falling over themselves to buy us drinks, and we only drink champagne. Last week, though, I was working on this cute fashion photographer. I asked him if he would like to shoot me & was gobsmacked when he replied that it would have to be from the waist up only as my thighs were too fat. Needless to say, I threw my champagne over him. So I was wondering if you could suggest to me a simple way of quickly slimming my thighs so that bozo can see how gorgeous I am and realize that he missed his chance?

With love,
Devon

Dr. Jackson says...

Dear Devon,

I suggest you learn my simple five-step plan for producing slim, sexy thighs. Then, if any bozo photographer has the nerve to refuse you because of your elephantine thighs, simply show him how to achieve perfect results in no time at all. Or, failing that, try keeping your jeans on.

Dr. B. Jackson

Before

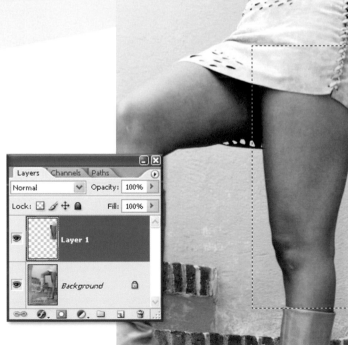

1 We shall start the thigh-slimming process by selecting the Rectangular Marquee tool **(M)** from the Toolbox. Click and drag across the right thigh to make a rectangular selection starting above the hem of the skirt and ending at the top of the boot. Now, press **Ctrl/⌘+J** to copy the selection onto a new layer, and then go to **Edit > Free Transform** or press **Ctrl/⌘+T** to apply the Free Transform bounding box to the new layer.

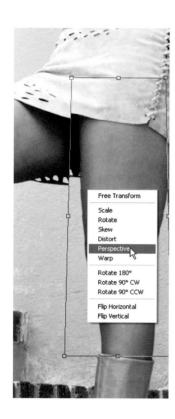

2 Right-click within the selection and choose **Perspective** from the pop-up menu. Now drag the top left handle of the bounding box to the right; as you do this you will see that the width of the top of the leg is reduced equally from both sides. When you are happy with the new thigh width, click on the tick symbol in the options bar or hit the **Return/↵** key to commit the transformation.

3 Return to the background layer and repeat the selection and transformation process with the left leg. This time, select the **Distort** option from the pop-up Transform menu and drag the bottom right handle of the bounding box upward until the hemline of the skirt matches with that of the right leg layer. Apply the transformation by double-clicking within the bounding box or by hitting the **Return/↵** key.

4 Return to the right leg layer and go to **Layer > Merge Down** or press **Ctrl/⌘+E** to merge the two leg layers together. Now that the thighs have been successfully slimmed down, all that is left to do is blend the new legs layer with the original layer. To do this, apply a layer mask to the legs layer by going to **Layer > Add > Layer Mask > Reveal All**.

5 Hit the **(D)** key to ensure that the default black and white foreground/background colors are selected, and then press the **(B)** key to select the Brush tool from the Toolbox. Now paint with black over the skirt and the join where the legs meet the boots to reinstate the background and blend the two layers seamlessly. When satisfied with the results of the layer mask, go to **Layer > Remove Layer Mask > Apply** and then use the Clone Stamp tool **(S)** to remove any

remaining unwanted areas of leg. Finally, compress the image by going to **Layer > Flatten Image** and show off your new improved slimmer thighs.

After

SLENDER ARMS
Trim and slender arms

Before

Dear Dr. Jackson,

Summertime is fast approaching and although I would dearly love to wear short-sleeved T-shirts and little cropped vest tops, I can't because I'm so self-conscious about my chubby arms. My friends tell me I should stop worrying and just get on with my life, but they wouldn't want to hurt me by telling me the truth. Every time I look at my arms in the mirror they seem to get chubbier.

I would greatly value your medical opinion on whether my arms really are chubby, and if so what can I do to make them slimmer? Or are my chubby arms just a delusional figment of my imagination?

Yours worryingly,
Helen

Dr. Jackson says...

Dear Helen,

If it's my honest opinion you're after, then I would say there are other things to worry about, such as "Are hair braids still in fashion?" or "Does that awful jewelry go with your outfit?" If you are still not convinced, try applying my procedure for turning stout, chubby arms like yours into beautifully trim and slender ones.

Dr. B. Jackson

P.S. That mirror of yours sounds fascinating. Did you get it from a fairground, by any chance?

1 This extremely quick method of removing unwanted fat from the arms can also be used on various other parts of the body, such as flabby thighs or a bulging midriff. The one thing this technique is dependent on, though, is a plain background. After opening the image you want to work on, press **(M)** to select the Rectangular Marquee tool from the Toolbox. Click and drag to create a rectangular selection around the girl's arm.

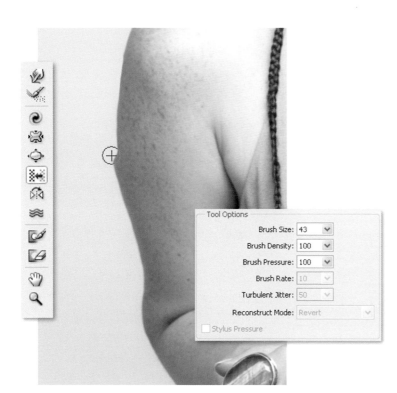

2 Now go to **Filter > Liquify** or press **Ctrl/⌘+Shift+X** to open the Liquify command interface. From the left toolbar choose the Push Left tool **(O)** and set the brush size to approximately 40 pixels. Position the cursor at the top of the arm, then click and drag the Push Left tool down the length of the arm. As you drag, you will see the background pixels shift to the right, instantly slimming the arm. Make sure you only drag the tool downward as this will push the background pixels to the right; if you drag the tool upward, the pixels in the arm will be pushed to the left, making the arm fatter instead.

3 You will find that you need a steady hand to smoothly drag the tool along the full length of the arm. Don't worry about this as you can use as many strokes as you wish. If you go wildly off line, the original undistorted image can be returned to at any time by clicking on the Restore All button. When you are happy with the reduction in size of the arm, click OK to apply the changes.

4 Although the outside edge of the arm now looks much slimmer, the inner edge near the elbow still looks a little flabby. To correct this, select the Lasso tool **(L)** from the Toolbox and draw a selection intersecting the inside of the arm. Next, press the **(S)** key to select the Clone Stamp tool, hold down the **Alt/⌥** key while clicking on the background to select a sample point, and clone the background over the flabby part of the inner arm. Finally, press **Ctrl/⌘+D** to deselect the selection and complete the look of the new slender arm.

After

SHAPELY CALVES AND ANKLES

Perfect pins

Dr. Jackson says...

Dear Dr. Jackson,

I have a real hang-up about my calves; they are really solid and muscular, which I feel is very unattractive in a woman. I hate my legs so much that I always wear jeans or trousers to hide them and would never dream of wearing a skirt. That was until recently, when my sister asked me to be a bridesmaid at her wedding. She made me wear a dress that came to the knee, showing off my chunky calves. I was so embarrassed I spent the whole wedding trying to find things to stand behind so that nobody could see my legs. Is there any simple technique that you could show me to reduce the width of my calves, which I could then apply to all the wedding photos so that I'm not reminded of my legs every time I look at the pictures?

Yours truly,
Suzanne

" Dear Suzanne,

Don't be embarrassed—just remember that old proverb, "Seldom seen, soon forgotten." I'm sure nobody will remember just how big your lower legs are, especially after a few glasses of champagne. My advice to you is to apply the following four simple stages to produce slimmer legs on all the wedding photos, and make sure you keep your trousers on in future.

The Doctor "

Before

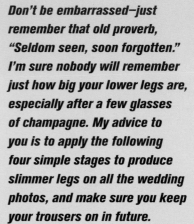

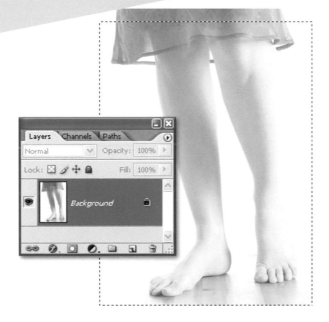

1 This surefire technique for slimming calves and ankles works especially well on any image where the subject is wearing a skirt, as it allows you to slim the legs while still keeping the skirt and upper body untouched and in proportion with each other. After opening your image in Photoshop, press the **(M)** key to select the Rectangular Marquee tool from the Toolbox, click on the left edge of the picture above the skirt hemline, and drag diagonally downwards to the bottom right corner of the picture, to create a selection encompassing the bottom 80% of the picture.

2 Right/control-click within the selection and choose Layer Via Copy from the pop-up menu (or press **Ctrl/⌘+J**) to copy the selection to a new layer. We will now begin the process of resizing the selection by pressing **Ctrl/⌘+T** to apply the Free Transform bounding box to the new layer. Hold down the **Alt/⌥** key and drag the center right handle inward to evenly slim the legs from both sides. When you are happy with the new leg width, press **Return/↵** to apply the free transformation results.

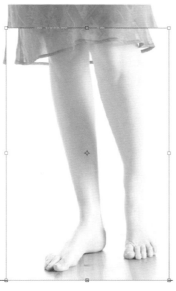

3 To apply a Layer Mask to the new layer, click on the Add Layer Mask icon at the bottom of the Layers palette or go to **Layer > Add Layer Mask > Reveal All**. Press the **(D)** key to ensure the default black and white background and foreground colors are selected, then press the **(X)** key to switch the foreground color to black. Next press the **(B)** key to select the Brush tool and paint over the orange dress with black to reinstate the original pre-squashed version. If too much of the top layer mask is removed and the edge of the original legs start to show through, hit the **(X)** key again to switch the foreground to white and paint over them to replace the mask.

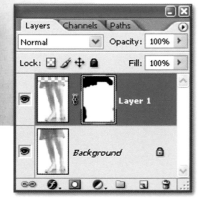

4 When reinstating the skirt via the layer mask, you will notice a fold in the skirt to the right has been duplicated. To remove this we will need to use the Clone Stamp tool, but first we must apply the layer mask by right/control-clicking on the mask in the Layers palette and choosing Apply Layer Mask from the pop-up menu. Now clone out the duplicate fold in the dress and any obvious joins in the flooring with the Clone Stamp tool **(S)** before merging the layers by pressing **Ctrl/⌘+E** to finalize the transformation from lardy legs to perfect pins.

After

SMALLER HANDS AND FEET
Delicate digits

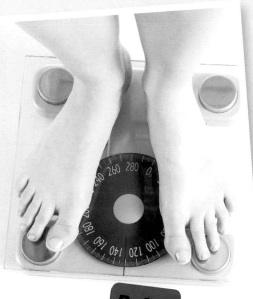

Before

Dear Photoshop Doctor,

For a woman I have extremely large feet. This causes me many problems when buying shoes as most ladies' styles don't go up to my size. I have to buy my shoes from specialist outsized shops that tend not to be very fashionable, or I just end up wearing men's trainers. I guess that there's no real surgical method of permanently shortening feet, but I'd be pleased if you could show me a Photoshop method which I could apply to my photographs. At least that way I could pretend I have small feet some of the time.

Yours truly,
Bobbi

Dr. Jackson says...

Dear Bobbi,

The techniques I use for reducing the size of extremities such as hands and feet are dependent on whether the extremity is photographed against a plain or detailed background. Therefore I have taken the liberty of including examples of both with my reply. So put your feet up and have fun applying my easy to follow techniques to your oversized trotters.

**Regards,
Dr. B. Jackson**

1 Reducing the size of these feet will be a slightly more complex task than the hands opposite, due to the busier background. Start by selecting the Magnetic Lasso tool **(L)** and trace around the outline of the left foot. Anchor points are automatically attached to the edge of the foot as you trace around it. If the line runs off course, press the **Delete** key while retracing the route to delete the anchor points one at a time. Join with the start point to complete the selection of the foot.

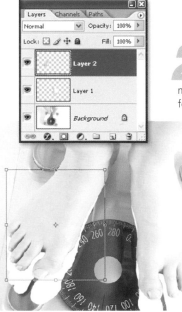

2 Right-click within the selection and choose Layer Via Cut from the pop-up menu to remove the selected foot from the background and place it on a new layer. Repeat the selection process with the right foot and place this on its own separate layer also. Press **Alt/⌥+T** to select the Free Transform tool and drag the handles to shorten the foot. When completely happy with the new size, press **Enter/↵** to apply the change and repeat with the left foot.

3 As you can see, the feet now look smaller but there are gaps in the background. We will remedy this by copying other areas of the background. Start by turning off both feet layers using the eye icons at the left side of each layer in the Layers palette. Click on the Background layer and use the Polygon Lasso tool **(L)** to make a selection of the dial between the feet. Press **Ctrl/⌘+J** to copy it to a new layer and then **Ctrl/⌘+T** to reposition the selection using the Free Transform tool. Carry on around the dial, copying sections to new layers and repositioning them until the dial is reconstructed. Press **Ctrl/⌘+Shift+E** to merge the visible layers and then use the Clone Stamp tool **(S)** to blend out any obvious joins.

4 Next use the Polygon Lasso to select the back legs of the scales; again, copy these to new layers and use the Free Transform command to reposition over the front legs. Merge the visible layers by pressing **Ctrl/⌘+Shift+E** and then use the Clone Stamp tool to clone the base of the scales over the missing sections. Now add a shadow under the feet layers by clicking on the Create New Layer icon at the bottom of the Layers palette and painting with black underneath the toes of each foot; lower the opacity of this layer to create a realistic shadow effect. Finally go to, **Layer > Flatten Image** to complete the size reduction.

After

Example 2

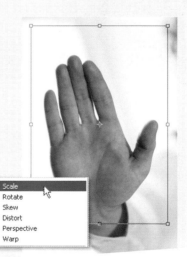

1 We will start by reducing the size of a hand that is against an almost plain background. After opening the image, press **(L)** to select the Lasso tool, and use this to draw a loose selection around the hand, making sure to include a good section of the background above and to the left side of the hand. Right/control-click within the selection and choose Layer Via Copy from the pop-up menu or press **Ctrl/⌘+J** to copy the selection to a new layer.

Deselect
Select Inverse
Feather...

Save Selection...
Make Work Path...

Layer via Copy
Layer via Cut
New Layer...

Free Transform
Transform Selection

Fill...
Stroke...

Last Filter
Fade...

2 Now go to **Edit > Transform > Scale** and drag the top left-hand corner of the bounding box diagonally downward. As you do this you will see the hand shrink. When the hand is the correct size, press the **Enter/⌐** key then use the Clone Stamp tool **(S)** to tidy up any obvious joins that may appear in the background. Make sure the Use All Layers box is ticked in the Tool Options bar, as this will allow you to sample from the background layer. Finally press **Ctrl/⌘+E** to merge the layers and view the completed smaller hand.

Scale
Rotate
Skew
Distort
Perspective
Warp

After

LONGER NECK
Stick your neck out

Dear Dr. Jackson,

Everybody I speak to hates at least one thing about his or her own body image. I wish I could say I was the exception to this, but unfortunately I can't. I don't yearn for the normal things like a smaller nose or bigger breasts; nothing so mundane for me. I wish I could have a longer neck. I know you are wondering why on earth anybody would want a longer neck. Well, to be honest, I think they look elegant and graceful and just wish I had a long slender neck myself. I don't think it is possible for me to physically lengthen my neck but I would be very pleased if you could show me how to achieve the look I desire on a photograph.

Many thanks,
Sam

Dr. Jackson says...

" **Dear Sam,**

Physical stretching of the neck is actually possible; the women of various African and Asian tribes have been doing exactly this for centuries with the aid of neck hoops. In your case, though, a far simpler way to achieve the results you require would be to follow my four simple stages to creating a longer neck without stretching your patience.

**Regards,
Dr. B. Jackson** "

Before

1 To begin this extremely simple technique for lengthening the neck, hold down the **Shift** key while pressing the **(L)** key three times to select the Magnetic Lasso tool from the Toolbox. Click on the top of the girl's head to lay down a start point, and then trace the outline of her hair to create a selection. As you do this, the Magnetic Lasso detects contrast changes between the foreground object and the background and lays down anchor points to define the edge of the girl's hair. If the selection wanders away from the hairline, remove the anchor points one at a time by backtracking along the selection while pressing the **Delete** key.

Feather: 1 px   ☑ Anti-alias   Width: 10 px   Edge Contrast: 10%   Frequency: 80

2 Carry on following the outline of the hair until you are roughly level with the bottom of the ears. Hold down the **Alt/⌥** key and click to temporarily change to the Freehand Lasso, then draw the selection across the hair to the line where the neck and the T-shirt meet. Let go of the **Alt/⌥** key to revert back to the

Magnetic Lasso and follow the neckline of the T-shirt. Hold down the **Alt/⌥** key and mouse-click once more to change back to the Freehand Lasso and draw the selection across the right side of the hair back to the hair outline. Revert back to the Magnetic Lasso and join up with the start point to complete the selection.

3 Now right/control-click within the completed selection border and choose Layer Via Copy from the pop-up menu to copy the selection to a new layer. Press the **(V)** key to select the Move tool from the Toolbox and then press **Up/↑** to nudge the selection up one pixel at a time, or hold down the **Shift** key and press **Up/↑** to nudge the selection

up ten pixels at a time. In this example I held down the **Shift** key and pressed **Up/↑** twice to move the selection up 20 pixels. Remember when elongating the neck to keep the effect to a minimum, as an overstretched neck will look false and unnatural.

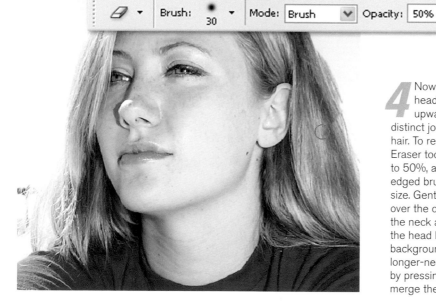

4 Now that the copy of the head has been moved upward, we can see a distinct join across the neck and hair. To remedy this, select the Eraser tool **(E)**, set its opacity to 50%, and choose a soft-edged brush 30 pixels in size. Gently run the Eraser over the obvious edges on the neck and hair to blend the head layer with the background. Complete the longer-necked version by pressing **Ctrl/⌘+E** to merge the layers together.

After

CONTENTS

SECTION 5

Pumping Iron

Dr. Jackson's classic bodybuilding techniques in the digital gymnasium

BULGING BICEPS
From mini to maxi

Dear Dr. Jackson,

There is a girl in my office I would really like to go out with. The thing is, she only goes out with beefy bodybuilder types, and I'm the opposite, thin and weedy. I know if she got to know me she would like me because I'm very kind, thoughtful, and polite. I would do anything to impress her. I have even become a member of my local gym—I go there at least three times a week and have been lifting weights to try and improve the muscles in my arms. Despite my obvious commitment and dedication I don't seem to be having much success yet. I was wondering if there are any formulas or compounds you could recommend. Please help me doctor—you are my last hope for wowing the girl of my dreams.

Yours in anticipation,
Jason

Dr. Jackson says...

Dear Jason,

If your "obvious dedication and commitment" only stretches to a handful of visits to the gym and I am your last hope, then I am afraid your impatience and obsession with this girl may have got the better of you. The only guaranteed way of adding muscle mass I can recommend is that you follow my four-part formula for bulging biceps and apply it to your own photographs. Then if you ever get the confidence to talk to this girl, you could always pretend you were once a bodybuilding champion.

Regards,
Dr. J

Before

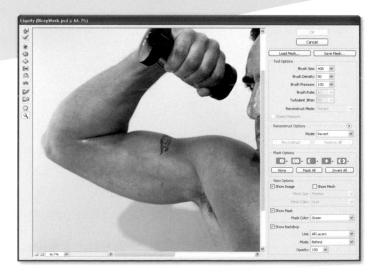

1 After opening the image you want to transform, open the Liquify command by going to **Filter > Liquify** (or by pressing **Ctrl/⌘+Shift+X**). When the Liquify interface appears, select the Zoom tool **(Z)** from the bottom of the toolbar and use it to zoom into the left arm by positioning the cursor over the arm and clicking.

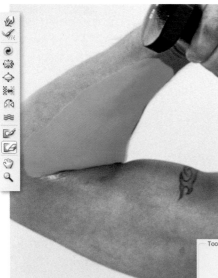

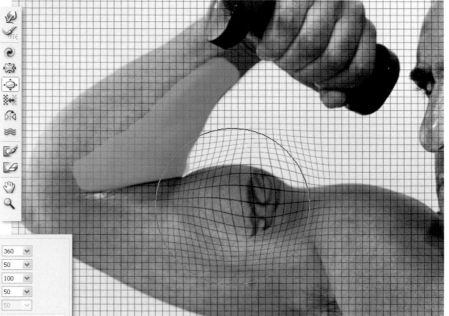

Tool Options
Brush Size: 360
Brush Density: 50
Brush Pressure: 100
Brush Rate: 50
Turbulent Jitter: 50
Reconstruct Mode: Revert
☐ Stylus Pressure

Reconstruct Options
Mode: Revert
[Reconstruct]   [Restore All]

Mask Options
◐ ◑ ◐ ◑ ◐
[None] [Mask All] [Invert All]

View Options
☑ Show Image   ☑ Show Mesh
Mesh Size: Large
Mesh Color: Blue

2 To increase the size of the muscle we shall be using the Bloat tool, but before that, select the Freeze Mask tool **(F)** from the toolbar. Use the Freeze Mask tool to paint over the forearm to prevent it from being affected by the muscle enlargement.

3 Now select the Bloat tool **(B)** from the toolbar and set the brush size to around 360 pixels. Turn on the Mesh by ticking the Show Mesh box in the View Options pane—this will give you a good indication of how the bloat effect is being applied to the image. Position the Bloat tool over the center of the bicep, click and hold down the left mouse button to watch it expand before your eyes.

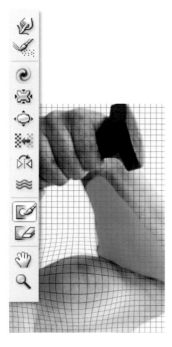

4 When you are happy with the size of the enlarged muscle, turn your attention to the right arm and repeat the process, making sure to freeze the forearm before expanding the muscle. Zoom out by clicking with the Zoom tool while holding down the key to make sure that both arms have the same amount of expansion applied, and then click OK to accept the change from weedy wimp to super-strong muscle man.

After

SHOULDERS
Stealing a super shape

Dear Photo Doctor,

My hero is the famous actor and kung fu expert Bruce Lee. Not only was he a superb actor and an unparalleled athlete but he also had the perfect body—lithe, muscular, and well toned. I know the chances of me ever having a body like that are pretty slim but it would be great if I could actually see what I would look like with a firm, well toned body. Are there any techniques you could show me to help me realize my dream? I have attached a rear-view picture in the hope that you could give me strong, firm shoulder muscles.

Many thanks,
Toby

Dr. Jackson says...

Dear Toby,

I'm sure after many devoted years of martial arts training, you too could have a body just like Bruce Lee's. But if you haven't got quite that much time to wait for your perfect body, I suggest you follow my six-stage tutorial to acquire strong, muscular shoulders and keep practicing your imaginary kung fu moves in front of the mirror.

**Kind regards,
Dr. B. Jackson**

Before

1 A great way of adding toned muscle to an otherwise muscle-free body is to cheat and borrow the muscles from another image. In this example we will take the shoulder muscles from a donor image and transplant them onto this weakling's muscle-free body. Start by opening the images in Photoshop. Maximize the window so that the picture is open nearly full screen. Select the Magnetic Lasso tool **(L)** from the Toolbox and drag around the outline of the back to make a selection of the back and shoulders. Now adjust the windows you're using so that you can see the recipient window too. Use the Move tool **(V)** to drag the selection onto the recipient image.

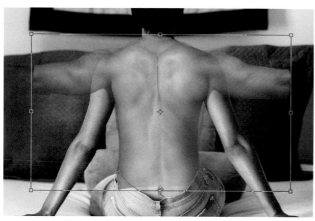

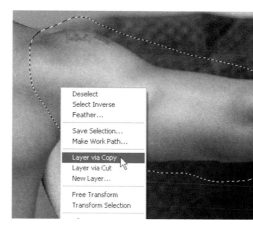

2 Maximize the screen of the recipient image and then lower the opacity of the back layer to about 60%—this will allow you to see through the layer to accurately position and resize the back to match that of the background image. Press **Ctrl/⌘+T** to open the Free Transform command and drag the bounding box handles to resize the back. Press the **Return/↵** key to apply the resize, then return the opacity of the layer to 100%.

3 Now that the size of the new back matches that of the background figure, you also need to reposition the arms. Use the Lasso tool **(L)** to make a rough selection around the right arm, right/control-click within the selection, and choose Layer Via Copy from the pop-up menu. Press **Ctrl/⌘+T** to apply the Free Transform bounding box to the selection, and drag the center pivot point to the left so that it is positioned over the center of the shoulder. Move the cursor outside the bounding box and you will see it change to a curved line with an arrowhead at each end. Hold the mouse button and drag downward to rotate the arm. Line the arm up with that of the recipient figure, then right/control-click within the bounding box and choose Distort from the menu. Drag the bottom right handle inward to match the edge of the arm with that of the recipient, and then press **Return/↵** to apply the change.

4 Return to the back layer and repeat this process with the left arm so that both the arms have been repositioned and placed on separate layers. Return again to the back layer and go to **Layer > Add Layer Mask > Reveal**. All this now allows you to remove the unwanted outstretched arms from the layer by using the Brush tool **(B)** to paint over them with black. Next, reduce the opacity of the brush and paint over the bottom of the back and the neck area to better blend them with the background figure.

5 Now apply an adjustment layer to the image by going to **Layer > New Adjustment Layer > Curves**. When the New Layer dialog box appears, tick Use Previous Layer to create a clipping mask box so that any color adjustments made apply only to the new back layer. Adjust the curves till the flesh tones of the new back layer blend seamlessly with the recipient figure. To complete the transformation, merge the layers using **Layers > Flatten Image**.

After

CHEST—BIGGER PECS
Chiseled chests

Dear Dr. Barry,

I'd love to have a toned muscular body but my busy schedule prevents me from devoting enough time to exercise. A good friend of mine recently had an operation to augment the pectoral muscles of his chest and the results look fantastic. He says it really wasn't that expensive and he was back at work after a week, with boosted confidence. I'm sure you will understand why this is such a big deal when I tell you that body image is vitally important to the type of company I keep. I am very interested in having the operation done as to me it sounds like the ideal way of getting the body I desire and deserve without having to spend all my time at the gym.

Yours anytime,
Simon

Before

Dr. Jackson says...

Dear Simon,

While pectoral implants may seem an attractive idea, the thought of possible hematoma, seroma, neurovascular injury, pnemothorax, hemathorax, and good old plain infection fills me with dread, not to mention how your body will look when you're 70, with two big lumps of silicone flapping around. My advice would be to apply my steps to some photographs, show the results to your friends, and keep your waistcoat on.

Kind regards,
Dr. Jackson

1 This technique for enhancing chest muscle mass is extremely easy and can usually be completed in a matter of minutes. Begin by opening the picture you want to improve, and then press **(L)** to select the Lasso tool from the Toolbox. Use the Lasso tool to make a rough rectangular selection around the left pectoral and then press **Ctrl/⌘+J** to copy the selection to a new layer. Double-click on the new layer text in the Layers palette and rename the layer "Left pec."

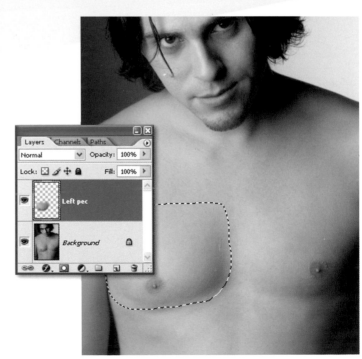

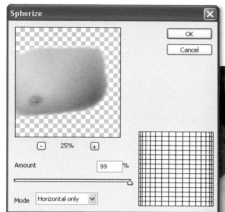

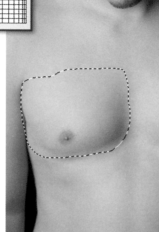

2 Now go to **Filter > Distort > Spherize** and choose Horizontal Only from the drop-down Mode menu. Move the amount slider as far as it will go to the right, and then click on the OK button to apply the distortion.

3 Return to the Background layer and use the Lasso to make a rough selection of the right pec. Press **Ctrl/⌘+J** again to copy the selection to a new layer, this time renaming it "Right pec." Now press **Ctrl/⌘+F** to apply the same settings of the Distortion to this layer.

4 Now that both pectoral muscles have been fully expanded, you need to realign them to properly fit the chest. Press **Ctrl/⌘+T** to activate the Free Transform tool and reposition each muscle on the chest. Double- click within the bounding box or press the **Enter** key to apply the changes. Press the **(E)** key to select the Eraser tool and erase around the edges of each muscle with a large soft brush to blend each layer with the background. When you are happy with the results of blending the layers, flatten the image by going to **Layer > Flatten Image**. Finally, press the **(O)** key to select the Burn tool. Set the range to shadows and the Exposure to 6% and apply a few strokes under the pecs to darken the shadows and make the muscles more defined.

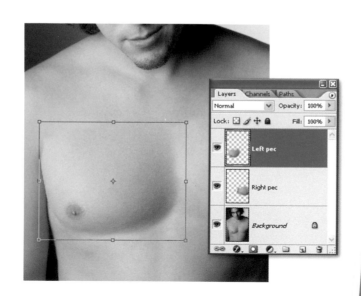

After

THE SIX-PACK STOMACH
From lardy to hardy

Dear Dr. Jackson,

I have heard about the body crafting techniques you use in your Digital Gym and was wondering if you could help me achieve my goal: a six-pack stomach. I am fit and healthy but also short of cash and very lazy, therefore I can neither afford the cost of a gym membership nor do I have the willpower to physically achieve my aim. I know a retouched photograph will not be an adequate substitute for the real thing, but if I can see the possible results it may spur me on to make the effort to start working out at home. I would be very grateful to you if you could find the time to show me how to achieve this result on a photograph of myself.

Yours sincerely,
Mark

Dr. Jackson says...

"

Dear Mark,

I can certainly show you how to achieve this look, but whether or not are able to make the minimal effort to apply my rudimentary five-point plan to your own photograph is quite another matter.

**Kind regards,
Dr. Jackson**

"

Before

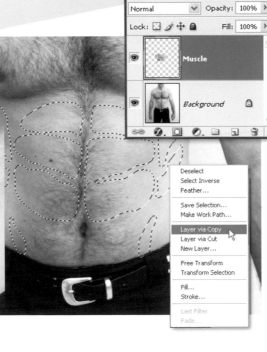

Deselect
Select Inverse
Feather...

Save Selection...
Make Work Path...

Layer via Copy
Layer via Cut
New Layer...

Free Transform
Transform Selection

Fill...
Stroke...

Last Filter
Fade...

1 To create the illusion of a six-pack stomach we will start by making selections of the areas where we want our defined muscle to be. It is useful to look at a photograph of a model with a six-pack as this will help in creating the right size, shape, and definition of the stomach muscles. Press **(L)** to select the Lasso tool and begin drawing the areas where you wish the muscle to be. Hold down the **Shift** key as you draw to add to the selection, or hold down the **Alt/⌥** key to subtract from the selection. When the selection is complete, control/right-click within it and choose Layer Via Copy from the pop-up menu.

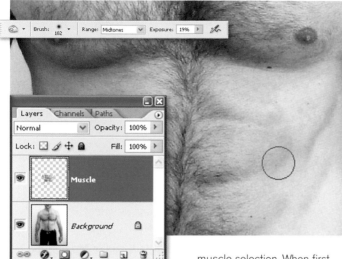

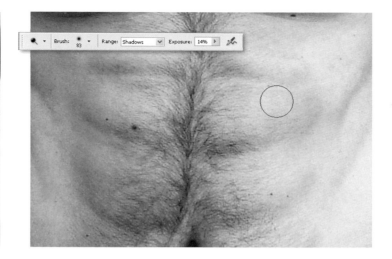

2 Select the Burn tool **(O)** from the Toolbox, choose Midtones from the drop-down Range menu in the Tool Options bar, and set the exposure to around 20%. Now gently apply the burn to the bottom and left edges of the muscle selection. When first applying the burn technique, it helps to turn off the background layer so that the muscle selection can be seen clearly. Using the Burn tool like this to darken the underneath of the selection gives the appearance of a shadow and adds definition to the muscle.

3 Return to the Tool palette and select the Dodge tool **(O)**. Set the Range to Midtones and the Exposure to around 10%. Gently brush over the tops of the muscle selections to add highlights to the muscle. As you can now see, the muscles are taking shape, but the love handles at each side of the stomach are still making it look a little bit flabby.

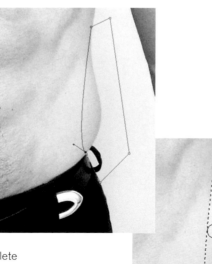

4 To remove the love handles, select the Pen tool, **(P)** make sure that the Paths option is selected, and select the background layer. Click with the Pen tool to start the path halfway up the torso. Reposition the cursor at the point where the edge of the trousers and the torso meet, and click and drag the mouse to curve the path into the torso. Complete the path roughly, then press **Ctrl/⌘+Return/↵** to convert the path into a selection.

5 Now select the Clone Stamp tool **(S)** from the Toolbox, choose a soft-edged brush, and then hold down the **Alt/⌥** key and click on the background within the selection to select a sample point. Clone over the area of the skin with the background. Only the area within the selection will be affected, so don't worry about going over the selection edge. Once done, press **Ctrl/⌘+D** to deselect and then repeat the process with the other side of the torso. Finally, merge the layers together by pressing **Ctrl/⌘+E** or by going to **Layers > Flatten Image** to reveal the finished washboard stomach.

After

LEGS AND THIGHS
Muscular legs without work

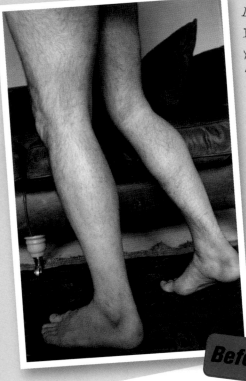

Dear Dr. Jackson,

I emigrated to Australia from the UK about ten years ago and it was the best decision I've ever made. Everything about my life here is far better than my old life. Every winter I can wind up my old workmates by sending them a Christmas card I've designed. This year I'm standing next to a barbecue on Bondi beach wearing swim shorts and a Santa hat while sipping an ice-cold beer. The caption reads "Merry Christmas lads, I'll chuck another shrimp on the Barbie for yas." This is sure to get a reaction. Although I'm happy with my design, my legs look a little bit puny in the photograph and I've decided to beef them up a bit. Can you give me any tips?

Regards,
Max

Before

Dr. Jackson says...

Dear Max,

It's nice to see that you are enjoying your new life, even if you haven't got Mel Gibson's legs. But don't worry, you can soon add a bit of meat to your scrawny thighs by following my simple four-stage procedure.

**Regards,
Dr. B. Jackson**

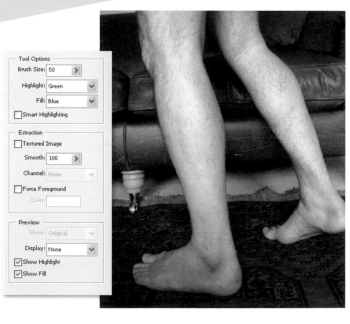

1 Before we can improve the leg muscles we must first extract the legs from their background, to ensure any distortions made are confined to the legs and do not affect the background. After opening the legs image, make a copy of it by dragging the layer onto the Create New Layer icon at the bottom of the Layers palette. Next go to **Filter > Extract** or press **Ctrl/⌘+Alt/⌥+X** to open the Extract command interface.

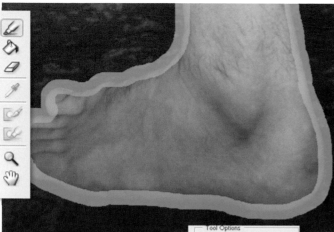

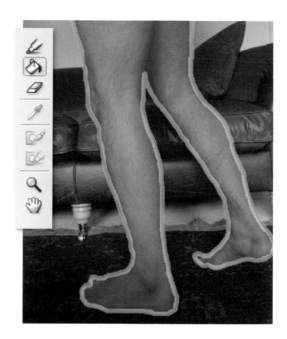

2 Use the Zoom tool **(Z)** to get closer to the legs and then select the Highlighter tool from the top of the toolbar. Set the brush size to 50 pixels and then trace the outline of the legs, ensuring both the foreground and background areas are covered by the highlighter. If you prefer, check the Smart Highlighting box; the highlighter then automatically detects the legs, edges as you draw around them, much like the Magnetic Lasso tool would. The

smart highlighting option can be temporarily disabled by holding down the **Ctrl** key as you drag the mouse. As we have zoomed into the image, we will need to hold down the **Space Bar** to temporarily select the Hand tool **(H)** and drag the mouse to move around the image in order to complete the outline of the legs.

3 Once the outline of the legs is completed, select the Fill tool **(G)** and click within the highlighted outline to fill the outline with a mask. Next click on the Preview button to watch the extraction take place. Use the Cleanup tool **(C)** and the Edge Touchup tool **(T)** to tidy up the edges of the extraction

before clicking OK to apply the extraction. If further tidying of the extraction is required, use the Eraser **(E)** to remove any unwanted remnants of the background, and the History Brush **(Y)** to paint back any areas of the legs accidentally removed by the extraction process.

4 Now that we have a cutout of the legs on a separate layer, we can use the Liquify tool to increase the leg muscles without affecting the underlying background image. Go to **Filter > Liquify** or press **Ctrl/⌘+Shift+X** to open the Liquify command interface. Use the Forward Warp tool **(W)** to drag out the muscular shape of the legs, and use the Bloat tool **(B)** to enlarge the muscles. Click OK to apply the changes and then press **Ctrl/⌘** to merge the layers and complete the image.

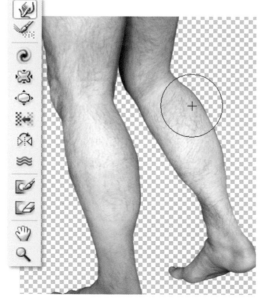

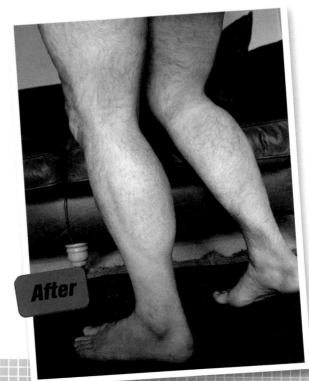

After

CONTENTS

SECTION 6

Radical Makeovers

Dr. Jackson's personal selection of
more in-depth case histories

NERD TO STUD
Ernest goes Arnie

Before

Hey Dr. Bee,

I need your help man, I dream of being a top rapper. I dig that whole scene, the money, the cars, the girls. I know I've got the talent to do it if only I had the chance. My problem is people don't take me seriously, just because I don't look like your typical rapper.

I'm very skinny and have a large Afro hairstyle, which I think looks cool and gives me an individual style, but I know if I send out pictures with my demo discs they won't even get listened to. So I've come up with this radical idea of mocking up a picture of myself to look like a typical gangsta rapper, all muscles, tattoos, and attitude. I thought it would be fun and it could greatly improve my chances of getting my demo heard.

Respect,
Leroy "Def" Star

Dr. Jackson says...

Dear Leroy,

I admire your willingness to retain your own distinctive style and only use stereotypical images to get yourself heard. If you truly have the talent to match your self-promotional ideas then I'm sure you will go far in the music industry—at the end of the day, originality will always triumph over conformity. To create your gangsta rapper alter ego and launch your career as a rap superstar, simply complete the following 11 stages and hope that the record companies believe the hype.

Good luck,
Dr. B. Jackson

1 Open the image you want to transform and immediately make a duplicate copy by dragging the background layer onto the Create New Layer icon at the bottom of the Layers palette. Then turn off the background layer by clicking on the eye icon to the left of the layer. You can now manipulate the image to your heart's content, safe in the knowledge that you have a copy of the original image to refer back to at any time. Now, to make distorting the figure easier, extract him from the background. Press **Ctrl/⌘+Alt/⌥+X** to open the Extract command interface and then check that the Smart Highlighting box is ticked in the Tool Options pane. Next, choose the Edge Highlighter tool **(B)** and use it to completely trace around the outline of the man. Make sure there are no gaps in the highlighted outline and then use the Fill tool **(G)** to apply a mask over the man.

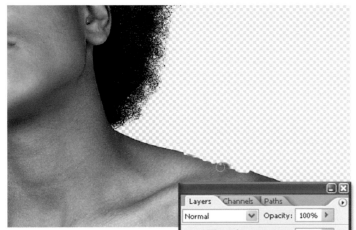

2 Click on the Preview button to remove the background and then use the Edge Touchup tool **(T)** to tidy the edges of the extraction before clicking OK to apply the extraction.Now go to the History palette and check the box next to the image state that reads Duplicate Image. Select the History Brush **(Y)** and go around the outline of the man, painting back any small areas of the figure that have been inadvertently removed by the extraction process (use the Eraser tool **(E)** to remove any areas of background that have been left behind).

4 Use a soft-edged Eraser **(E)** to blend the neck area with that of the background copy layer below, and then click on the background copy layer and remove any sections of the arms and shoulders that may be peeping out from behind Layer 1. Once this has been done, return to Layer 1 and press **Ctrl/⌘+E** to merge the layer with the Background copy layer.

3 Press the **(L)** key to select the Polygonal Lasso tool from the Toolbox and make a rough selection around the body of the figure, but do not include the head within the selection. Press **Ctrl/⌘+J** to paste a copy of the body to a new layer, then go to **Edit > Free Transform** (or press **Ctrl/⌘+T**) to apply the Free Transform bounding box to the copied selection. Right-click within the bounding box and choose the Perspective option from the pop-up menu. Now drag the top right corner handle to the right to increase the width of the man's shoulders. When you are happy with the width of the shoulders, hit the **Enter/Return** key to apply the transformation.

5 Now that we have changed the basic physique of the man, we can turn our attention to building up muscle mass around the arms and shoulders. Go to **Filter > Liquify** or press **Ctrl/⌘+Shift+X** to open the Liquify command interface. Select the Forward Warp tool **(W)** from the top of the toolbar and set the brush size to around 260 pixels. Now go around the outline of the figure, pushing out the edges of the skin to give the impression of a muscular body. When happy with the results of the distortions, click OK to apply the changes and return to the main Photoshop interface.

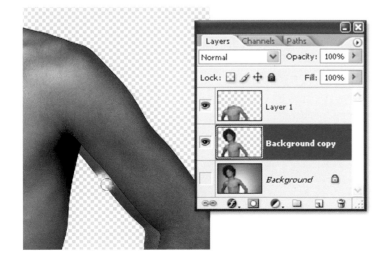

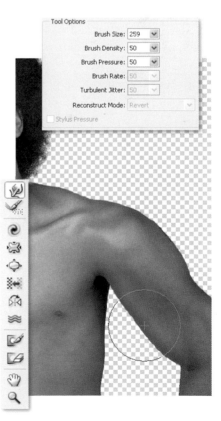

6 Now adjust the chest muscles by making a selection around both pecs, copying the selection to a new layer by right/control-clicking within the selection, and choosing Layer Via Copy from the pop-up menu. Next press **Ctrl/⌘+T** for Free Transform. Hold down **Alt/⌥+Shift** as you drag the right-side handle to proportionally increase the width before hitting **Return/↵** to apply the transformation. Now use a soft-edged Eraser tool **(E)** to remove the edges of the selection so that it seamlessly blends with the Background copy layer. Then use the Burn tool **(O)** with the range set to shadows and the exposure set at 8% to darken the underside of the chest muscles before pressing **Ctrl/⌘+E** to merge the layer with the background.

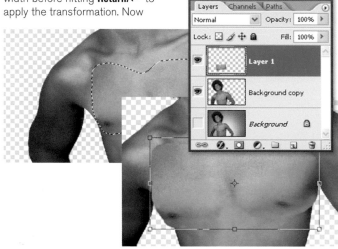

8 Now that we have created the perfect body it is plain to see that Leroy's funky Afro doesn't quite fit the gangsta image we would like to portray, so we will now change it to a more suitable cropped style. Click on the camera icon at the bottom of the History palette to make a snapshot of the present image state, and then check the box to the left of the new snapshot to set the source point for the History brush. Now use the Eraser **(E)** to remove the hair, leaving the new, cropped style. If too much of the hair is accidentally removed, simply use the History brush **(Y)** to paint back the hair.

7 You can now create the illusion of a six-pack stomach by making selections of the areas where you want your defined muscle to be with the Lasso tool **(L).** Next, copy the selections to a new layer by right/control-clicking within the selection and choosing Layer Via Copy from the pop-up menu. Gently use the Burn tool **(O)** to darken the underside of the muscles, and the Dodge tool **(O)** to slightly lighten the tops of each muscle. It may also be necessary to add a small amount of Gaussian blur to the selection to soften the muscle edges, and lower the layer opacity to better blend with the background before merging the layers. Now to complete the new improved body: use the Dodge and Burn tools again on the arm and shoulder muscles.

9 With his new cropped hairstyle and beefy toned body, Leroy's new look is starting to take shape. All we need to do now is apply a few essential accessories. We will start this process by adding a few tattoos to the body. Select the Custom Shape tool **(U)** and choose Leaf 2 from the drop-down shape menu. Click on the color box to open the Color Picker dialog box and select a dark blue color. Create the shape and press **Ctrl/⌘+T** to use the Free Transform tool to reposition the shape over the arm. Now convert the vector shape into a bitmap shape by going to **Layer > Rasterize > Shape**; this will allow the shape to be freely edited with the Eraser tool. Use the Eraser tool at low opacity to soften the shape and then go to **Filter > Noise > Add Noise** and adjust the amount slider to 10%. Next go to **Filter > Blur > Gaussian Blur** and apply a pixel radius of 0.5% to the tattoo. To complete the

tattoo effect, choose the Darken blend mode from the drop-down Blending mode menu and reduce the layer opacity to 80%. Repeat this process to apply a number of different tattoos to the body.

10 No gangsta rapper look is complete without some bling, so we will now add a chunky gold chain around our man's neck. Open your chain image and use the Magnetic Lasso tool to select the chain, press **Ctrl/⌘+C** to copy the selection, and then return to the image and press **Ctrl/⌘+V** to paste the chain onto a new layer.

Press **Ctrl/⌘+T** to apply the Free Transform bounding box to the chain and then drag the handles to resize and reposition the chain around the man's neck. Tidy up the edges of the chain with the Eraser **(E)** and then go to **Layer > Layer Style > Drop Shadow** to open the Layer Style dialog box and apply a drop shadow to the chain.

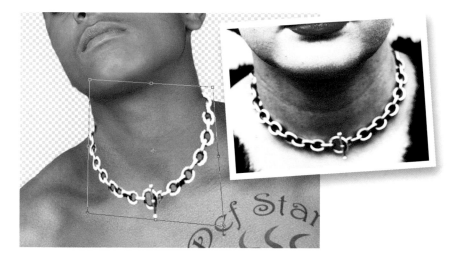

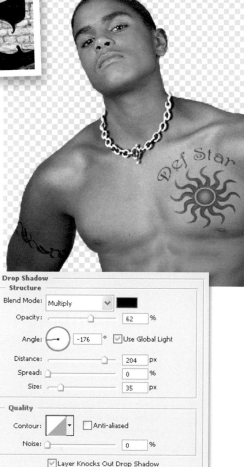

11 All we need now to complete our image is a suitable background. Here we've found a wall image and used the Move tool **(V)** to drag the image onto the picture. Position the image below the Background copy layer in the Layers palette to create a background. Next, click on the Background copy layer to make it active, and go to **Layer > Layer Style > Drop Shadow** to open the Layer Style dialog box and apply a drop shadow to our man. Adjust the angle, opacity, and distance of the shadow until it looks realistic and then hit OK to complete the change from drippy dreamer to gangsta rapper.

After

BEAUTY AND THE BEAST
Creating catwoman

Dear Dr. Jackson,
I'm pretty sure that you will think I am completely mad after hearing my request, but what the hell! At least mad is better than boring. I would like you to turn me into a cat. I know you can't really do this—I'm not that crazy—but I would like you to blend a picture of me with that of a cat.
I firmly believe in reincarnation and I'm convinced that in a previous life I was once a cat. I've always had a strange affinity with cats, I'm very independent but can also be very affectionate when I want to be, I hate dogs, and my favorite food is fish.
Yours faithfully,
Kim

Dr. Jackson says...

Dear Kim,

Please don't tell me you chase mice and do your business behind the sofa or I will definitely think you're mad. I have completed your request and included a straightforward how-to guide so that you can reincarnate yourself as any animal you think you may have once been. As for thinking you were once a cat because you like fish, I'm not so sure. I like cowboy movies, but that doesn't mean I used to be Billy the Kid.

Kind Regards,
Dr. Barry Jackson

Before

1 To successfully create any form of animal/human hybrid it is important to retain the distinguishing features of each subject so that they will still be recognizable once the image has been completed. It is no good just pasting a cat's head on top of a woman's body and calling it catwoman, as that won't impress anybody. Before you start on your image, decide which features from each subject you want to keep and then work toward that aim. In this example I had already decided I would like to keep the girl's hair, eye shape, mouth, and clothes, and the cat's pupils, ears, nose, and whiskers, which when successfully blended together, would result in a realistic cat/woman crossbreed. Now that our objective has been decided on, we can begin the process of creating our new image by first opening both the pictures of the woman and the cat in Photoshop.

2 Click on the cat image to make it active, then select the Elliptical Marquee tool from the Toolbox by holding down the **Shift** key and pressing the **(M)** key. Click and drag across the pupil of the cat's left eye to make a circular selection around it. Don't worry about making the selection too precise, as we will be removing the edges of the selection later. Now select the Move tool **(V)** from the Toolbox and drag the selection from the cat image window onto the woman image window to create a new layer. Double-click on the layer name and rename the layer "Left pupil."

3 The pupil is too big for the woman's eye, so to resize it go to **Edit > Free Transform** (or press **Ctrl/⌘+T**) to apply the Free Transform bounding box around the pupil. Hold down the **Shift** key as you drag the bottom right corner of the bounding box inward to scale the pupil proportionally. Reposition the pupil over the pupil of the woman's left eye and then hit the **Return/↵** key to apply the distortion and remove the Free Transform bounding box.

4 Select the Eraser tool **(E)** and use a soft-edged brush to gently run around the outside of the pupil to soften the edge. Then choose the Hard Light blending mode from the drop-down blend modes menu at the top of the Layers palette to blend the pupil with the eye below. Now repeat the selection, transform, and repeat the blending process with the right eye.

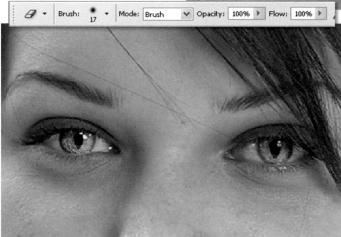

5 Return to the cat image window and press the **(L)** key to select the Freehand Lasso tool from the Toolbox. Draw a rough selection around the face of the cat and then drag the selection onto the woman image window with the Move tool **(V)**. Rename the layer "Face," and then reduce the layer's opacity to 50%. Press **Ctrl/⌘+T** to apply the Free Transform bounding box to the layer and reposition and resize the cat's face to correspond with the woman's face below.

6 You can now blend the cat's face with that of the woman by way of a Layer Mask. Click on the Create New Layer Mask icon at the bottom of the Layers palette to apply a mask to the 50% opacity face layer. Press the **(D)** key to ensure the default black and white foreground/background colors are selected, and press the **(B)** key to select the Brush tool and paint with black over the areas of the cat's face layer you wish to remove. Once you have removed most of the unwanted areas, return the opacity of the face layer to 100% and fine tune the mask by pressing the **(X)** key to switch between black to remove the mask and white to replace it. As you work, press the **[** key to reduce the brush size for intricate areas, and the **]** key to increase the brush size for larger areas.

7 When you are happy with the results of the mask, permanently apply it to the layer by right-clicking on the mask icon in the Layers palette and choosing **Apply Layer Mask** from the pop-up menu. Now patch the area above the left eye where the cat's eye used to be by selecting the Freehand Lasso tool **(L)** and drawing a rough selection around the area. Move the selection up so that it is positioned over a suitable area of fur, right/control-click within the selection and choose Layer Via Copy from the pop-up menu. Use the Move tool **(V)** to reposition the new fur patch layer over the space above the eye, and then press **Ctrl/⌘+E** to merge it with the face layer. Repeat this process with the right eye to complete the fur face layer.

8 Return to the cat image window and use the Freehand Lasso tool **(L)** to make a rough selection of the right ear. Drag it onto the woman image window with the Move tool **(V)** and then press **Ctrl/⌘+T** to apply the Free Transform bounding box. Resize and reposition the ear over the woman's head and press **Return/↵** to apply the results. Now use a soft-edged Eraser **(E)** to tidy up around the ear and blend the ear into the hair. Repeat this process with the left ear.

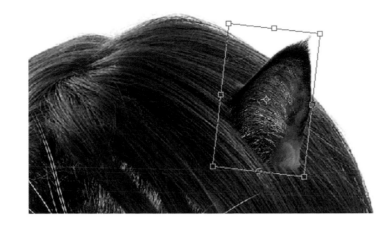

9 Now that the face has been covered with fur we need to do the same with the neck and arms. Repeat the selection, transform, and mask process we used on the face to apply fur to the neck and arms. When the neck and arms have been successfully covered with fur, turn off the background layer and then press **Ctrl/⌘+Shift+E** to merge the visible fur layers together. Turn the background layer back on and then blend the fur layer with the background layer via the Hard Light blending mode. Finally, use the Burn tool to selectively darken the fur, adding shadows around the chin and hairline before pressing **Ctrl/⌘+E** to flatten the image and complete the amalgamation of cat and woman.

GIRL TO BOY
A real tomboy

Dear Dr. B. Jackson,

My husband and I have a wonderful six-year-old daughter whom we couldn't be happier with. She is extremely intelligent and loving and we both love her deeply, even though she can also be a little madam and a drama queen to boot. We have often thought that it would be nice to provide her with a little brother as a playmate but we are not so sure that we would like to return to sleepless nights and the changing of nappies. That said, we are very intrigued to know what our son might look like. We would appreciate it if you could create a visual representation of how you would envisage our son looking at six years old.

Yours faithfully,
Monika

Dr. Jackson says...

Dear Monika,

As discernible male and female facial features are not fully formed on younger children, the successful transformation from a girl into a boy or vice versa is not always dependent on simply altering the face. Other factors such as hairstyle and clothing are far more important and should always be addressed. I just hope you won't be too disappointed if your son turns out to be another daughter.

Kind Regards,
Dr. Barry Jackson

Before

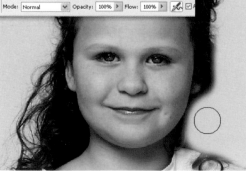

1 Once opened in Photoshop it is plain to see that the most distinguishable female feature of our image is the long hair, so to begin our gender swap operation we will first create a more boyish style. As the girl has been photographed against a plain background there is no need to first isolate the girl from the background; we can simply clone the background over the hair to change the style. Press the **(S)** key to select the Clone Stamp tool from the Toolbox and then choose a large brush from the Tool Options bar. Hold down the **Alt/⌥** key as you mouse-click on the plain background to select a sample point, reposition the cursor over the girl's long hair, and paint to clone the background over the hair. As you get nearer to the face, reduce the size of the brush by pressing the **([)** key. Zoom into the face with the Zoom tool **(Z)** and carefully trace around its outline.

2 Once the hair has been shortened, our next job is to replace the center parting with a more boyish quiff. To do this, first select the Lasso tool **(L)** and draw a selection around the front right section of the girl's hair. Now press **Ctrl/⌘+J** to copy the selection to a new layer, followed by **Ctrl/⌘+T** to apply the Free Transform bounding box to the copied selection. Use the Free Transform command to reposition and stretch the selection over the center parting of the hair to create a quiff and then hit the **Return/↵** key. Press the **(E)** key to select the Eraser tool, choose a soft-edged brush, and erase around the edges of the quiff to blend with the background hair.

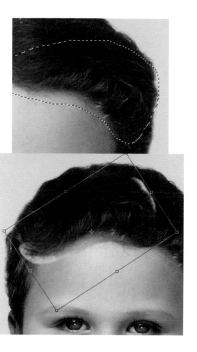

3 As you can now see, simply changing the girl's hairstyle has already given her a much more boyish appearance, but there is still more we can do to complete our transformation. So we shall continue by duplicating the left ear and using it to replace the right ear, which is still partly covered with long hair. Select the Rectangular Marquee tool **(M)** and make a selection around the left ear. Press **Ctrl/⌘+J** to copy the ear to a new layer, go to **Edit > Transform > Flip Horizontal** to flip the ear over, and then press **Ctrl/⌘+T** to apply the Free Transform bounding box to the ear. Reposition the new ear over the right ear and press the **Return/↵** key to apply the change. Lower the opacity of the ear to 50% and use the Eraser tool **(E)** to blend the edges with the background layer.

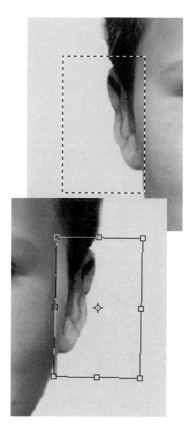

4 Next we will make a few simple changes to the face, starting with the eye color. Return to the background layer and ensure the colors are the default black and white. Next, press the **(Q)** key to enter Quick Mask mode, and the **(B)** key to select the Brush tool. Paint with black over the pupils of the eyes to apply a semi-transparent red mask over the eyes. Press the **(Q)** key again to return to standard mode, and then press **Ctrl/⌘+Shift+I** to reverse the selection. Now press **Ctrl/⌘+U** to bring up the Hue/Saturation dialog box, tick the Colorize box, and adjust the Hue and Saturation sliders to change the eye color. Cick on **OK** to apply the change and **Ctrl/⌘+D** to deselect the eyes.

5 We will now apply some freckles to our subject. Click on the foreground color to bring up the Color Picker dialog box and select a middle shade of brown as the new foreground color. Click on the Create New Layer icon at the bottom of the Layers palette to create a new layer above the background. Use a one-pixel sized Brush **(B)** to paint a random pattern of dots across the nose and cheeks, then go to **Filter > Blur > Gaussian Blur** and apply a one-pixel radius blur to the freckles. To complete the adjustments to the face, return to the Background layer and, with the Burn tool **(O)** range set to Shadows and a low Exposure, brush over the eyebrows to darken them.

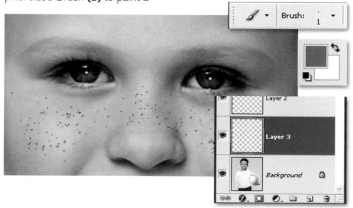

6 With the face and hair now complete, we can turn our attention to changing the style of clothes from a girl's to a boy's. Use the Clone Stamp tool **(S)** to clone over the sequined flowers on the T-shirt top, making sure you select sample points close to the area to be cloned over, so that the color and tone of the cloned area blend into the surrounding area. Next, alter the neckline of the T-shirt by using the Lasso tool **(L)** to make a section of the T-shirt including the neckline. Copy this to a new layer by pressing **Ctrl/⌘+J**, reposition the selection with the Free Transform tool, and use the Eraser **(E)** to blend with the background.

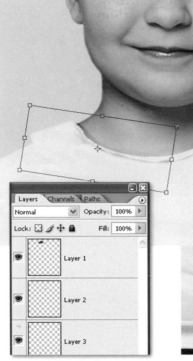
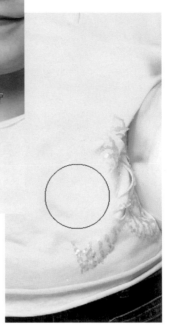

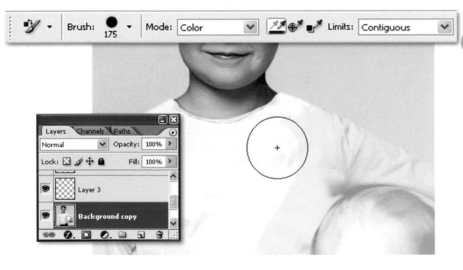

7 We will now change the color of the T-shirt by selecting the Color Replacement tool **(J)** from the Toolbox. Go to the Tool Options bar and set the Mode option to Color and the Sampling option to Continuous. Select white as the foreground color and then paint over the T-shirt with the Color Replacement tool to change the color of the T-shirt from baby blue and yellow to a more neutral white. Once the T-shirt has been recolored, change the pocket design on the jeans by using the same techniques used to alter the T-shirt.

8 We will now add a simple design to the T-shirt to help confirm our subject's gender as a boy. Select the Custom shape tool from the Toolbox and choose the man shape from the drop-down shape menu in the Tool Options bar. Hold down the mouse button as you drag it across the T-shirt to create the shape. Press **Ctrl/⌘+T** to apply the Free Transform bounding box to the shape and reposition it over the center of the T-shirt. Next, select the Type tool **(T)** and add the slogan "Men Only" to the bottom of the man shape. Rasterize both the shape and the type layer by right-clicking on the respective layers and choosing Rasterize from the pop-up menu. Then merge the shape and type layers together.

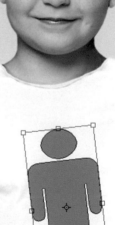

9 Use the Liquify tool to distort the shape of the design to match the undulations of the T-shirt, and then blend it with the T-shirt via the Multiply layer blending mode. To finish our transformation from girl to boy we will replace the colorful beach ball with a battered old soccer ball. Open your soccer ball image and click on the white background with the Magic Wand tool **(W)**. Invert the selection by pressing **Ctrl/⌘+Shift+I** and then use the Move tool **(V)** to drag the ball onto the image of the child. Lower the opacity of the ball to 50% and use the Free Transform tool **Ctrl/⌘+T** to resize and reposition the ball over the beach ball. Go to **Layer > Add Layer Mask > Reveal All** and paint with black over the ball to reveal the hand and any areas of the T-shirt that cover the ball.

10 Right/control-click on the layer mask and choose the Apply Layer Mask option from the pop-up menu to apply the results of the mask to the ball layer. Click on the Create New Layer icon at the bottom of the Layers palette to add a new transparent layer above the ball layer. Select the Brush tool **(B)** and use a soft-edged brush to paint in some shadows around the ball. Finally, flatten the image by going to **Layer > Flatten image** to complete the transformation from girl to boy.

After

MAN TO WOMAN
Brother to Sister

Before

Dear Dr. B. Jackson,

Lately I've been thinking a lot about my long-lost twin sister Serena. We were only five years old when my parents separated. I stayed with my father in New York while Serena moved to Canada with my mother. At first we kept in touch but as the years passed by we eventually lost contact. I recently tried to reach her at her old address in Toronto, but it transpires she moved to Europe about ten years ago and her new address is unknown. We were still children when we I last saw her so I can't help thinking about what she would look like now as an adult. As children we were very much alike, so I have enclosed a picture of myself for reference.

Yours faithfully,
Simon

Dr. Jackson says...

Dear Simon,

I'm sure that as you are twins your sister will still look much like you, but perhaps with slightly softer features and, most probably, without the beard. I have completed a projection of how I feel Serena will look now, and included a step-by-step walkthrough of how I achieved this result, in case you would like to apply the techniques used in this example on other pictures.

**Kind regards,
Dr. Barry Jackson**

1 We will begin our gender swap operation by first removing the facial hair from our image. Use the Zoom tool **(Z)** to zoom into the mouth area of the image and then select the Clone Stamp tool **(S)** from the Toolbox. Go to the Tool Options bar, choose a soft-edged brush, and set the Mode to Lighten. Hold down the **Alt/⌥** key and click on an area of smooth skin close to the moustache to create a sample source point. Now click on the moustache to clone the sample over the moustache. Setting the blend mode to Lighten ensures only the areas darker than the source point are cloned over, which means the facial hair will be removed without affecting the lighter skin areas. Carry on cloning to remove the rest of the moustache and the beard; always sample as close to the clone area as possible so that color and tone of skin match the surrounding area.

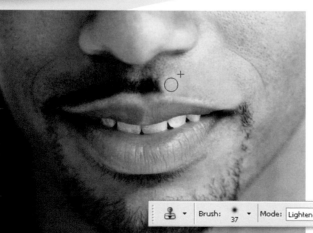

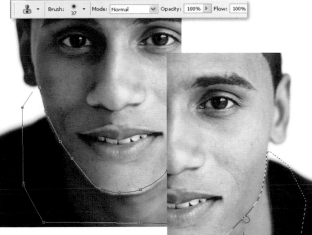

2 Now that the facial hair has been removed, we can see that we need to redefine the jawline to make it more feminine. Select the Pen tool **(P)** from the Toolbox. Click on the left side of the face to start the path, which will run slightly inside the existing jawline to create a smoother, more angular, feminine look. Return to the start point and click to close the path, right/control-click within the path, and choose Make Selection from the pop-up menu. Select the Clone Stamp tool **(S)** again and clone the neck area over the section of chin contained within the selection. Press **Ctrl/⌘+D** to deselect and view the new jawline.

3 We shall now turn our attention to the nose, which needs to be reduced in length and width and straightened up slightly. Press the **(L)** key to select the Freehand Lasso and draw a rough selection around the nose, making sure to include a good proportion of each cheek in the selection. Press **Ctrl/⌘+J** to copy the selection to a new layer and then press **Ctrl/⌘+T** to apply the Free Transform bounding box to the new layer. Right-click on the bounding box, choose Skew from the pop-up menu, and then drag the bottom left corner of the bounding box inward to straighten up the nose. Right- click again on the bounding box and this time choose Perspective from the pop-up menu. Drag the bottom left corner of the bounding box inward this time to reduce the width of the nose. When satisfied with the results. press **Return/↵** to accept the changes.

4 Use a soft-edged Eraser **(E)** to gently remove the edges of the duplicate nose layer so that it blends with the background, then press **Ctrl/⌘+E** to merge the layers. Now that the nose has been straightened and reduced in width it still looks quite long, since our subject has got quite a long face. Rather than just reduce the length of the nose, we will shorten the whole face slightly. Select the Rectangular Marquee tool **(M)** from the Toolbox and make a selection of the top half of the head. Press **Ctrl/⌘+J** to copy to a new layer and then press **(V)** to select the Move tool. Now press the down arrow on the keyboard to move the top of the head downward. When you are happy with the reduction in the length of the face, use a soft-edged Eraser **(E)** to blend any obvious edges with the background before pressing **Ctrl/⌘+E** to merge the layers.

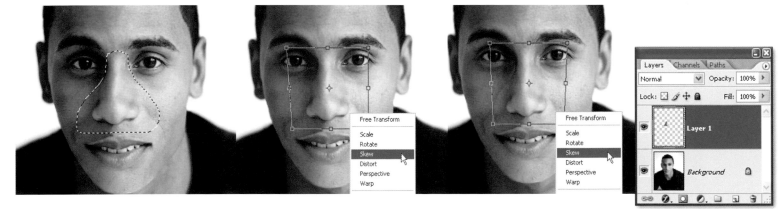

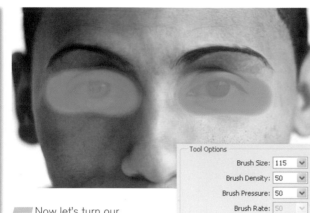

5 Now let's turn our attention to trimming and shaping the eyebrows. Press **Ctrl/⌘+Shift+X** or go to **Filter > Liquify** to open the Liquify interface. Use the Freeze Mask tool **(F)** to paint a green mask over the eyes; this will prevent them from being distorted by any changes we make to the eyebrows. Select the Pucker tool **(S)** and drag it across the eyebrows to slim them down. Next use the Forward Warp tool **(W)** to push the center of the eyebrows upward to arch them. While still in Liquify mode, use the Bloat tool **(B)** to make the eyes slightly larger. When satisfied with the distortion results, click **OK** to apply the changes.

6 As you can now see, the face is starting to take on a more feminine appearance, but we still have more to do before our man convincingly becomes a woman. Press the **(L)** key to select the Freehand Lasso tool and draw a selection around the right eye. Press **Ctrl/⌘+J** to place the eye on a new layer and then press **Ctrl/⌘+T** to apply the Free Transform bounding box to the eye, right-click within the box, and choose distort from the pop-up menu. Now push the bottom right handle upward to make the eye slightly slanted. Press **Return/↵** to apply the change and then repeat with the left eye. Next use the Smudge tool **(R)** to drag out individual eyelashes to lengthen them.

7 Now that all the prominent facial features have been sufficiently changed, we can concentrate on the skin. Merge both the eye layers with the background layer, then make a duplicate copy of the background layer by dragging the layer onto the Create New Layer icon at the bottom of the Layers palette. Next, go to **Filter > Blur > Gaussian Blur** and drag the blur radius slider to the right until the skin in the preview pane is suitably softened. Click **OK** to apply the blur to the copy layer and then check the Set History Source box next to the final state at the bottom of the History palette. Now click on the next state up, which should read Duplicate Layer, and you will see the image is returned to its previous state before the blur was applied. Press the **(Y)** key to select the History Brush, set the opacity to around 50%, and paint over the areas of skin that require softening to selectively reinstate the blurred layer.

8 Zoom into the mouth area and use the Clone Stamp tool **(S)** to reduce the gaps between the teeth and then use the Magnetic Lasso tool **(L)** to make a selection around the teeth. Now press **Ctrl/⌘+U** to open the Hue/Saturation dialog box and drag the Lightness slider to the right to lighten the teeth. Click on **OK** to apply the change and then use the Magnetic Lasso tool **(L)** again, this time to make a selection of the lips. Press **Ctrl/⌘+J** to copy the lips selection to new layer and then open the Hue/Saturation dialog once more by pressing **Ctrl/⌘+U**. Drag the Hue slider to the left to add a pink color to the lips and drag the saturation slider to the right slightly to boost the color.

9 Although the face has now been transformed, the overall effect is diminished by the manly bulk of the body and the severely short hairstyle. To remedy this, we will first use the Clone Stamp tool **(S)** to reduce the size of the shoulders by cloning the background over them. Now, use the Rectangular Marquee tool **(M)** to make a selection of the neck of the T-shirt top and and use the Free Transform tool to drag the neck down to elongate the V-shape. We will now borrow a woman's cleavage from another picture to add to our image. Open a suitable image and use the Rectangular Marquee tool **(M)** to select the cleavage, use the Move tool **(V)** to drag the selection onto our image to create a new layer, then reduce the opacity of the layer to 50%. Press **Ctrl/⌘+T** to apply the Free Transform bounding box to the cleavage, then resize and reposition the cleavage over the V-neck of the T-shirt. Hit **Return/↵** to apply the transformation and use the Eraser tool to blend the cleavage with the background before returning the opacity back to 100%.

10 To complete our transformation, we will now use the same borrowing technique to apply a new hairstyle. Open the picture from which you wish to take a hairstyle, and make a selection of the head. Drag the head selection onto your image to create a new layer and reduce the opacity of the layer to 50%. Then use the Free Transform tool to resize the head so that the eyes of the head layer are positioned above the eyes of your image. Hit the **Return/↵** key to apply the new size and then choose **Add Layer Mask > Reveal All** from the Layer menu to add a Layer mask to the layer. Carefully paint with black over the mask to reveal the image beneath, and paint with white to hide the image beneath. Adjust the mask until you are satisfied with the look of the new hairstyle. Finally, flatten the image by going to **Layers > Flatten Image** to reveal the female counterpart to the male we started with.

After

ARTIFICIAL YOUTH
Twenty-five years younger

Dear Dr. B. Jackson,

Under my pseudonym, I am a popular writer of romantic fiction, but although I am well known through my writing and have a very large number of literary fans, I have managed to remain unrecognizable to the public. As my alter ego is meant to be approximately 25 years younger than me, I would like to keep it that way. My problem is that my publishers are putting increasing pressure on me to include a photograph of myself on the back cover of each of my novels; they claim that the fans are demanding a face to identify with. So because of this I was wondering if you could create a visual representation of "me the author" by taking 25 years off an image of myself.

Yours sincerely,
Paula

Before

Dr. Jackson says...

Dear Paula,

How could I refuse such a succinctly expressed request? Surely the whole reason for writing fiction is to create characters, therefore is it not appropriate that the author of your books should also be a character created from a version of yourself? I hope you find the enclosed younger version of yourself suitable for fooling your public.

Kind regards,
Dr. Barry Jackson

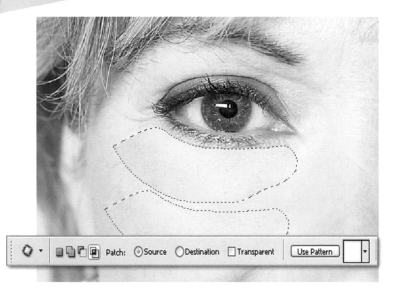

1 As bags and crows' feet around the eyes are the biggest giveaway to Paula's age, we will start the rejuvenation process by replacing these with smooth skin, to instantly provide a more youthful appearance. Hold down **Ctrl/⌘+Space Bar** as you click and drag a selection around the left eye to zoom into the eye. Press the **(J)** key to select the Patch tool, make sure the radial Source button is checked in the Tool Options bar, and then draw a selection around the wrinkled skin under the eye. Now drag the patch selection onto a smooth skin area of the cheek to replace the wrinkles with smooth skin.

Fade

Opacity: 57 %   OK

Cancel

Mode: Normal

☑ Preview

2 Repeat the bag removal process on the right eye and then hold down the **Shift** key as you press the **(J)** key twice to select the Healing Brush tool. We will now use this to completely remove the remaining lines and wrinkles from around the eyes. Hold down the **Alt/Opt** key and click to sample a smooth area of skin close to the line you wish to remove. Now brush over the line and the sampled skin area will be blended over it, replacing the line. If you want to soften the line without completely removing it, select Fade Healing Brush from the Edit menu or press **Ctrl/⌘+Shift+F** to open the Fade dialog box, then adjust the slider to apply the desired amount of healing to the line.

3 Carry on using the Healing Brush to remove the lines around the mouth and along the cheek and chin, and then duplicate the layer by pressing **Ctrl/⌘+J**. We will now soften the skin to remove any texture associated with older-looking skin. Go to **Filter > Blur > Gaussian Blur** and enter a radius value of 3 pixels in the pop-up Gaussian Blur dialog box. Click OK to apply the blur to the duplicate layer. Now apply a layer mask to the blurred layer by going to **Layer > Add Layer Mask > Hide All**. This adds a black mask to the layer, completely obscuring the blurred layer and allowing the background layer below to show through.

Gaussian Blur

OK

Cancel

☑ Preview

— 50% +

Radius: 3.0 pixels

Layers Channels Paths

Normal   Opacity: 100%

Lock: ☒ ✎ ✛ 🔒   Fill: 100%

Layer 1

Background

4 Press the **(D)** key to ensure the default black and white foreground/background colors are selected, and then press the **(B)** key to select the Brush tool. Right/control-click to open the brush picker, choose a large soft-edged brush, and then adjust the opacity to 30% in the Tool Options bar. Press the **(X)** key to make the foreground color white and then paint over the nose, cheeks, and chin of the face to remove the mask, revealing the blurred layer and softening the skin. Make sure you don't paint over the eyes, hair, or mouth as these need to remain sharp and in focus. If any of these areas are painted over by mistake or too much of the blurred layer is revealed, simply press the **(X)** key to switch the foreground color to black and paint the mask back in.

Hue: 43

Saturation: 25

Lightness: 0

5 When you are happy with the skin softening, right/control-click on the mask icon in the Layers palette and select Apply Layer Mask from the pop-up menu. Then merge the layers by pressing **Ctrl/⌘+E**. Now we can turn our attention to brightening the eyes to give them a youthful sparkle. Select the Magnetic Lasso tool **(L)** from the Toolbox and draw around the pupil of the left eye to make a selection. Hold down the **Shift** key to enable you to add to the selection and then draw around the pupil of the right eye. Now press **Ctrl/⌘+U** to open the Hue/Saturation dialog box, tick the Colorize box, and adjust the Hue and Saturation sliders to make the eyes a natural green color. Click OK to apply the change and deselect the pupils by pressing **Ctrl/⌘+D**.

6 Next, use the Magnetic Lasso tool **(L)** to select the whites of the eyes. Press **Ctrl/⌘+U** again to open the Hue/Saturation dialog box, but this time drag the Lightness slider slightly to the right to brighten the eyes. Don't be tempted to overdo the lightness adjustment, as this will leave the eyes looking too bright and unrealistic. Now that the eyes are refreshed, we can turn our attention to the mouth. Repeat the selection and brightening process with the teeth, remembering not to lighten them too much.

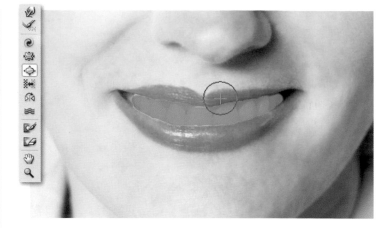

7 As the lips tend to get thinner with age, we will now increase the size of the top lip to make the mouth fuller and more youthful. Select the Liquify option from the Filter menu to open the Liquify interface. Use the Zoom tool **(Z)** to zoom into the mouth area and then use the Freeze Mask tool **(F)** to paint over the teeth to protect them wile we enlarge the lips. Now select the Bloat tool **(B)** and brush over the lips to pump them up a little. When happy with the enlargement, click OK to apply the distortion and return to the standard Photoshop interface.

8 To complete the lips we will adjust the lipstick color to a younger, plummy shade and add some lip gloss to give them more shine. Use the Magnetic Lasso tool to make a selection of the lips and then press **Ctrl/⌘+J** to paste the lip selection to a new layer. Now press **Ctrl/⌘+B** to open the Color Balance dialog box and adjust the color sliders to produce the desired shade of lipstick. Click OK to apply the changes to the new lip layer. Now go to **Filter** > **Artistic** > **Plastic Wrap**, adjust the sliders to apply the desired amount of highlight, detail, and smoothness to the effect, and then click **OK** to apply the results.

9 Although Paula's face is now much more youthful and radiant, her hairstyle is a little too old for a young woman. To remedy this we will give her a much more youthful, short, choppy look. Use the Freehand Lasso tool **(L)** to cut into the hair and create the choppy look on the left side of the head. Try to follow the natural flow of the hair as much as possible. Select the Clone Stamp tool, hold down the **Alt/⌥** key to sample the background, and then clone the background over the hair. Next, select a section of the hair. Copy it to a new layer by pressing **Ctrl/⌘+J** and reposition and resize it with the Free Transform tool. To thicken the hair, use a soft-edged Eraser to blend the edges into the hair. Repeat this process a few times to layer the hair, creating a strong, youthful look.

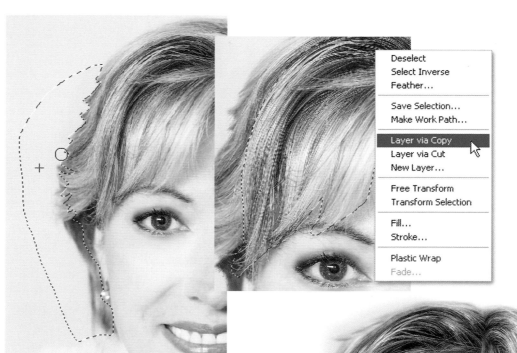

10 To complete the hair, select the Smudge tool **(R)**, set the brush size to two pixels, and go around the edges of the hair dragging out hairs. Then hold down the **Shift** key and press the **(R)** key to select the Blur tool. Set the opacity to 40% and run around the outside of the hair to soften the edges. Flatten the image by going to **Layers > Flatten Image**, then use the Dodge tool **(O)** to selectively highlight sections of the hair, creating a multi-tonal highlighted effect that completes our transformation from mother to daughter.

After

ARTIFICIAL AGING
Youth to senior citizen

Dear Dr. Jackson,

Could you please help me make my point? My girlfriend is convinced that when I get older I will look just like my father. I've told her no way—my dad is nearly bald, the little remaining hair he does have is gray, and his face is heavily lined. I look after my hair; I've always used quality shampoo and conditioner and I moisturize my face daily. I intend to mature with age like a f ine wine, as opposed to my dad who's aging like a moldy old cheese. I would be much obliged if you could create a photographic projection of what I will look when I'm in my late fifties to settle the argument once and for all.

Yours faithfully,
Brian

Dr. Jackson says...

Dear Brian,

There are only three things certain in life— death, taxes and the effects of aging. Fine lines around the eyes and mouth become deeper and more obvious, the skin around the eyes begins to sag, the lips become thinner, and I'm afraid to say that if your father is bald then there is every chance that you will also lose your hair. I have completed my projection on your image and include a detailed "how to" guide. If I were a betting man I'd go with your girlfriend.

**Good luck,
Dr. Barry Jackson**

Before

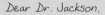

1 As hair loss is an extremely common occurrence in older men, we will begin our aging process by receding the hairline. Before you start to manipulate the image, make a duplicate copy of it by pressing **Ctrl/⌘+J**, so that any adjustments you make to the image are confined to the copy,

leaving the original untouched. Now hit the **(M)** key to select the Elliptical Marquee tool and make a selection of the forehead without encroaching into the hairline. Right/control-click within the selection and choose Layer Via Copy from the pop-up menu to place the forehead selection onto a new layer.

2 Now press the **(V)** key to select the Move tool and reposition the forehead selection over the hair to give the impression of a balding head. Press the **(E)** key to select the Eraser tool, right-click and choose a large, soft-edged brush from the brush picker. Carefully erase the bottom edge of the new forehead to blend the layer smoothly with the background image.

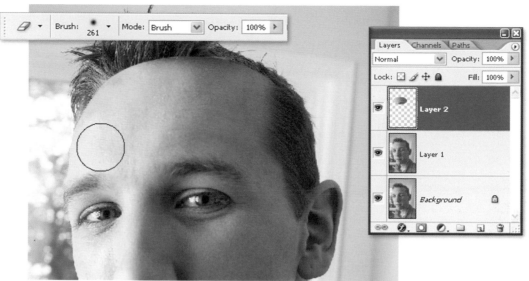

3 Return to the copied background image by clicking on it in the Layers palette, and then select the Clone Stamp tool **(S)** from the Toolbox. Carefully clone the background over the remaining hair to create the appearance of a convincing bald head. As our copied forehead layer is above the layer we are currently cloning, we can easily copy the background without affecting the dome of the bald head. When you are happy with the results of cloning the background, click on the copied forehead layer and press **Ctrl/⌘+E** to merge the layer with the background layer.

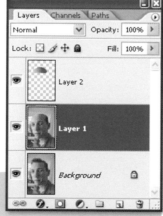

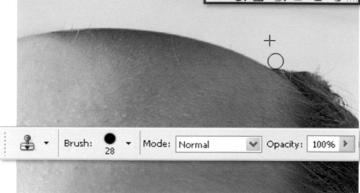

4 Although the bald head instantly adds ten years to our subject, he has still got firm, youthful skin, which stops him from looking too old. To remedy this we will now use the Liquify tool to drag down the skin, which will add to the aging process. Press **Ctrl/⌘+Shift+X** or go to **Filter > Liquify** to open the Liquify interface, use the Zoom tool **(Z)** to zoom into the face, and then the select the Forward Warp tool **(W)** from the top left of the tool palette. Use this to drag down the skin over the eyes to make the eyelids more hooded, and the skin below the eyes to create larger bags. Also drag down the skin around the mouth, and as men's ears tend to get larger as they age, drag down the earlobe to enlarge it. When you are happy with the distortion results, Click **OK** to apply the changes and return to the main Photoshop workspace.

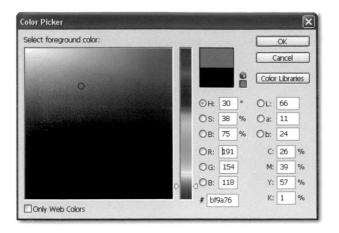

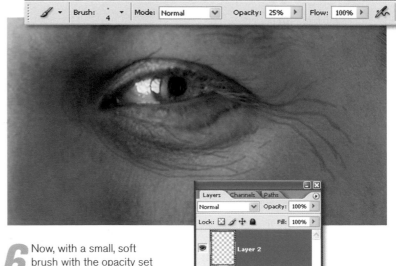

5 We will now use the Brush tool to draw some wrinkles onto the face. Rather than painting directly onto our image, we will paint these onto a new layer that can be applied to the face later, when we are satisfied with the results. Click on the Create New Layer icon at the bottom of the Layers palette to add a new transparent layer above our image, and then select the Brush tool **(B)** from the Toolbox. Click on the foreground color in the Toolbox to open the Color Picker and take a sample color from the wrinkles under the eyes. Click OK to set it as the foreground color.

6 Now, with a small, soft brush with the opacity set to around 25%, liberally draw wrinkles around the eyes and mouth and across the forehead. Putting the wrinkles on a separate layer means we can easily remove the lines we don't want with the Eraser, without affecting the image underneath.

Use a soft-edged Eraser **(E)** set to low opacity to selectively soften the lines and blend them with the background image.

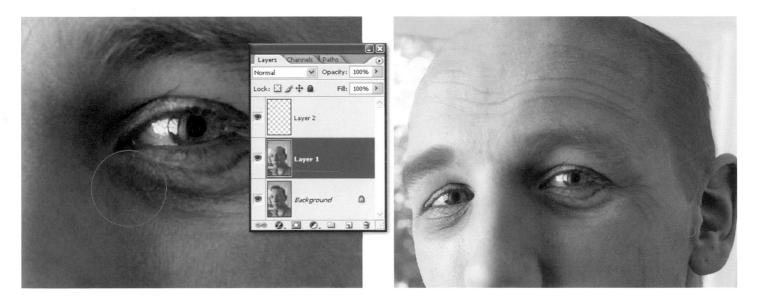

7 Once you are satisfied with the results of the wrinkle layer, return to the background layer and select the Burn tool **(O)** from the Toolbox. Go to the Tool Options bar and choose a large, soft-edged brush. Set the range to midtones and the exposure to 6%. Now use the Burn tool to darken the areas around the eyes and mouth and trace the lines of the wrinkle layer to emphasize the wrinkles more.

8 Now that the face has been aged sufficiently, we need to gray the hair slightly to complete the aging effect. Press the **(Q)** key or click on the Edit in Quick Mask Mode icon at the bottom of the Toolbox, select the Brush tool, and then press the **(D)** key to change the foreground and background colors to the default black and white. Now paint with black to apply a quick mask over the hair and eyebrows.

9 Hit the **(Q)** key again to return to standard mode and turn the mask into a selection. Press **Ctrl/⌘+Shift+I** or choose Inverse from the Select menu to invert the selection, and go to **Image > Adjustments > Hue/Saturation** or press **Ctrl/⌘+U** to open the Hue/Saturation dialog box. Adjust the Lightness slider to +25 to gray the hair, and click OK to apply the change. Now select the Eraser tool **(E)**, choose a soft-edged brush at low opacity, and run around the edges of the hair and eyebrows to blend with the background image. Then lower the opacity of the layer to 80% to create a more natural look.

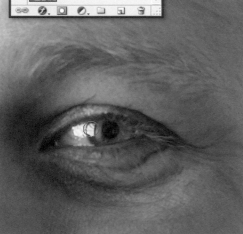

10 To complete the older look, select the Sponge tool **(O)**, set the mode to desaturate and the flow to 50%, and gently brush over the pupils to remove some of the youthful color from the eyes. Next, use the Brush tool **(B)** set to low opacity to draw individual hairs sprouting from inside the ears and nose. Finally, flatten the layers by going to **Layer > Flatten Image** to complete our father-from-son image.

After

GLOSSARY

ABDOMINOPLASTY The "tummy tuck"—reshaping the abdomen by removing excess skin and fat through up to five hours of surgery.

AUGMENTATION MAMMAPLASTY Or "boob job." There are actually various procedures common today. Saline-filled silicone shells inserted underneath breast tissue are the norm in the US, where silicone-filled implants are banned. String implants are less common but continue to grow after surgery, so are favoured by "adult entertainers." Finally, doctors are starting to experiment with tissue-engineered implants that combine a scaffold material with the patient's own cells.

ALPHA CHANNEL While each color channel defines the level of a certain color for each pixel, this channel defines the level of transparency for each pixel, allowing you to create images with objects of varying levels of transparency. A layer mask might be thought of as an alpha channel for its layer.

ANTI-ALIASING The smoothing of jagged edges on diagonal lines by giving intermediate color values to pixels. Commonly used on text.

ARTIFACT Any flaw in a digital image, such as the "noise" created by using a low-quality mode in a digital camera.

BACKUP A copy of either a file or a program in case the original becomes corrupted or is accidentally lost.

BIT DEPTH The number of bits per pixel (usually per channel, sometimes for all the channels combined), which determines the number of colors that pixels can display. Eight bits per channel is needed for photographic-quality imaging (8 computer bits can hold up to 256 shades; 256 x 256 x 256 = 16.8 million possible colors).

BITMAP Technically an image composed of pixels—small squares—which are either black or white, but typically used to describe any pixel-based image, whatever the bit depth.

BLEPHAROPLASTY Eyelid surgery performed by making incisions along the natural lines of the eyelids.

BOTOX The popular trade name for the potent neurotoxin known to scientists as Botulinum toxin. It has found uses in both biological warfare and cosmetic treatment, as it blocks nerve impulses.

CHANNEL In digital imaging, a channel is one of the primary colors used to make up an image. These are typically red, green, and blue (RGB), though alternatives such as CMYK are used by professionals.

CMYK Cyan, magenta, yellow, and "key" (black) are the channels used in traditional "process" printing. The three colors are the purest forms of the three primary colors you mixed paints with at school, and a separate black compensates for the technical problems in mixing a pure black.

COLLAGEN INJECTIONS Used as a lip enhancement, collagen is the main component of ligaments and tendons, with a great tensile strength. The injected filler can come from the patient's own fat or skin, or from donated tissue.

COLOR PICKER An on-screen palette of colors you can pick from in your image editor.

COMPRESSION The technique of rearranging digital data so that it occupies less space (in terms of megabytes) on media, and to reduce transfer times on the Internet. Compression can be simply mathematical, or it can be "lossy," sacrificing some data such as fine details. This is how the JPEG image format works.

DOTS PER INCH (DPI) A unit of measurement used to represent the resolution of output devices such as printers. Used correctly, it refers to the dots of the various inks the printer uses (usually four), and not the pixels of an image (usually millions of shades), but even professional designers confuse this. The correct term for a digital image file is pixels per inch (ppi).

EXTRACT A process in image editing where a selected part of an image is removed from the area around it. Typically, a subject is "extracted" from its background to be placed on a new one.

EYEDROPPER In Photoshop, a tool for gauging and selecting the color of pixels.

GIGABYTE Approximately one billion bytes, or 1,024 megabytes—this is the usual measure of hard disk sizes. By comparison, an ordinary recordable DVD holds 4.3GB.

GRADIENT In image editing, this is a smooth transition from one color tone to another.

HISTOGRAM A "map" of the distribution of tones in an image, arranged as a graph. The horizontal axis is 256 steps from dark to light, and the vertical axis is the number of pixels. In a dark image, for example, there will be taller bars for the darker shades. A large area of the same tone will produce a spike.

JPEG Aside from being a corruption of fictional nurse Jane Peg's name, JPEG is a compressed (qv) file format designed to store pictures. It allows variable levels of quality loss in exchange for ever-smaller file sizes.

LIPOSUCTION (or Suction-assisted Lipectomy). Literally sucking fat cells from the body with a tube and vacuum device.

MASTOPEXY The raising of sagging breasts by removing skin from the upper part of the breast and, possibly, placing it beneath in order to give a more pleasing contour.

MEGAPIXEL More of a marketing term than a technical one, this is simply the number of pixels on a camera's sensor chip, measured in millions. So, a chip with 1,280 x 960 sensor cells (1,228,800 pixels) would be called 1.2 megapixels.

MIDTONES The range of tonal values in an image anywhere between the darkest and the lightest, usually referring to those approximately halfway.

PIXEL A corruption of Picture Element, this is the smallest unit of any digital image. Essentially tiny squares making up a grid, each with a color assigned to them by the computer or camera. The color will have a numeric value (see Bit Depth), and their size is determined by the file's pixels per inch (qv) setting.

PIXELS PER INCH A measure of resolution for a bitmapped image. 72ppi, for example, means for each inch there will be 72 pixels, or for each square inch 72 x 72 = 5184. For printing purposes, 300ppi is more common (90,000 per square inch) so it's easy to see why megapixels (qv) are important on digital cameras.

PLASTIC SURGERY The general term for surgery performed for aesthetic reasons. The word "plastic," in this context, derives from the Greek *plastikos*, meaning to mould or shape, and not modern plastics, despite a common perception that this is the case.

RAM Random Access Memory. This is the working memory of the computer, to which the processing chip has direct access. The more RAM your computer has, the faster it will work, since the data the processor needs can be kept available to it to access very quickly.

RGB Red, green, and blue. From the perspective of digital cameras, televisions and monitors, these are the primary colors. They form the "additive" model of color, in that they mix to form white (as opposed to paints, which subtract from white).

RHINOPLASTY Cosmetic surgery conducted on the nose. It was pioneered by Jacques Joseph in the 19th century, and involves moving and shaping cartilage for either cosmetic effect or to facilitate breathing.

SOFTWARE Computer programs which enable the computer to perform tasks. This includes operating systems (like Windows or Mac OS) as well as job-specific applications (like Photoshop).

THUMBNAIL A small representation of an image, usually used to identify the image from a large collection in a browser.

TIFF Tagged Image File Format. A standard and popular graphics format. Typically this is used by printing professionals as it does not, by default, compress images, and so does not risk losing data. However it is a "tagged" format, which means it is flexible: some programs have added support for various forms of compression, and Photoshop even allows you to save its layers. Not all programs can understand all TIFF tags, so use these extensions cautiously.

TOOLBOX Photoshop's Toolbox normally appears to the left of the image window, enabling you to have access to all the most frequently used tools. If you accidentally close your Toolbox, use the **Window > Tools** menu option to bring it back.

TOOL OPTIONS BAR Once a tool has been selected from the Toolbox, Photoshop's Tool Options Bar provides access to the main tool-specific options. This typically appears at the top of the Photoshop window, though it can be moved.

TRANSPARENCY A degree of transparency applied to a pixel so that you can see through it when the image or layer is used in conjunction with others. TIFFs define transparency as an alpha channel (qv), but not all file formats allow for transparency.

VECTOR GRAPHICS Images made up of mathematically defined shapes, such as circles or rectangles, or complex paths (lines) built up of mathematically defined curves or corners. Vector graphics can be displayed at any size or resolution without loss of quality, but they lack the tonal subtlety of bitmapped images. Photoshop's Pen tool makes use of vector path layers.

ZOOM TOOL In image editing tools it's often impossible to see all the pixels of an image onscreen at once, so they can be scaled down. Equally they can be "zoomed" for close work, perhaps to the point that one pixel in the image uses many more on the display. Where possible, try and work at 100% to get the most accurate preview on your monitor.

INDEX

Acknowledgments

Useful URLs

Every person photographed and used in this publication is a model and their image is used for illustrative purposes only.

Thanks to Justine Caine for so convincingly playing the role of Nurse Jane Peg.

Thanks to my good friend Neil Hickson for taking the photographs of myself as Dr. Jackson.
www.neilhickson.co.uk

Adobe Inc.
Suppliers of Photoshop and Photoshop Elements, leading graphics applications.
www.adobe.com

Apple Computer
Check for the latest news on Macintosh Computers, Aperture photography software and, of course, the ubiquitous iPod.
www.apple.com

Corel
Latest product news on Paint Shop Pro, a popular Photoshop alternative, and Painter.
www.corel.com

Digital Photography Review
Continuously updated photography news site, offering exceptionally detailed reviews of new cameras, a database of reviews from 1995, forums and more. Don't buy a camera without checking out this site.
www.dpreview.com

Extensis
Supplier of the popular Portfolio application for ordering, cataloging and copyrighting photographs.
www.extensis.com

LaCie
If your computer's hard drive is getting full, look no further for an excellent range of storage solutions.
www.lacie.com

Nixvue
If your memory card isn't large enough, have a look here.
www.nixvue.com

Wacom
Famous in the world of graphics tablets, Wacom's technology helps make digital editing more natural.
www.wacom.com